ROGUES & HEROES

Library and Archives Canada Cataloguing in Publication

Butler, Paul, 1964-
Rogues & heroes of the island of Newfoundland / Paul Butler and
Maura Hanrahan.

Includes bibliographical references and index.
ISBN 1-894463-73-0

1. Newfoundland and Labrador--Biography. 2. Newfoundland and
Labrador--History--Miscellanea. I. Hanrahan, Maura, 1963- II. Title.
III. Title: Rogues and heroes of the island of Newfoundland.

FC2155.B88 2005   971.8'0099   C2005-902257-4

PRINTED IN CANADA

FLANKER PRESS LTD.
ST. JOHN'S, NL, CANADA
TOLL FREE: 1-866-739-4420
WWW.FLANKERPRESS.COM

We acknowledge the financial support of the Government of Canada through the Book
Publishing Industry Development Program (BPIDP) for our publishing program.

 Canada Council   Conseil des Arts
for the Arts   du Canada

We acknowledge the support of the Canada Council for the Arts
which last year invested $20.3 million in writing and publishing throughout Canada.

We acknowledge financial support from the Government of Newfoundland
and Labrador, Department of Tourism, Culture and Recreation.

ROGUES & HEROES

OF THE ISLAND OF NEWFOUNDLAND

PAUL BUTLER
and
MAURA HANRAHAN

FLANKER PRESS LTD.
ST. JOHN'S, NL
2005

ACKNOWLEDGEMENTS

We would like to thank: the Centre for Newfoundland Studies at Memorial University; the Maritime History Archive at Memorial University, the National Archives of Canada; the Canadian Coast Guard; the Grenfell Historical Association; the Heritage Foundation of Newfoundland and Labrador; Library and Archives Canada; the Smallwood Heritage Foundation; the A.C. Hunter Library, especially the Newfoundland Room; the Provincial Archives of Newfoundland and Labrador; Flanker Press; the Writers' Alliance of Newfoundland and Labrador; the Twillingate Museum; Hawthorne Cottage (home of Captain Bob Bartlett), Brigus; Alasdair Black of Admiralty House Museum and Archives, Mount Pearl; Dr. Philip Hiscock, Department of Folklore, Memorial University; Shane Kelly; Dr. Elizabeth Miller; Nurse Myra Bennett Foundation, Daniel's Harbour; CBC Radio, St. John's; the Colony of Avalon, Ferryland; the Harbour Grace Museum; the Mary March Museum, Grand Falls–Windsor; *The Telegram*, St. John's; *The Beaver*, Winnipeg; the *Worker's Voice*, St. John's; and all the Newfoundland writers who have gone before us.

For Vanessa

TABLE OF CONTENTS

Introduction xiii

1. An Accidental Discovery 1
   JOHN CABOT

2. Prince of Pirates 6
   PETER EASTON

3. Newfoundland's Elusive Princess 12
   SHEILA NAGUEIRA

4. New World Entrepreneur 18
   LADY SARA KIRKE

5. Outside the Law 23
   PETER KERRIVAN AND THE MASTERLESS MEN

6. A World-Famous Prophet 29
   RICHARD BROTHERS

7. A Fighting Spirit 35
   DEMASDUIT

8. Last of the Beothuk? 40
   SHANAWDITHIT

9. South Coast Heroine 44
   ANN HARVEY

10. The Last Woman Hanged 50
    CATHERINE SNOW

11. Making this Place Our Own 56
    WILLIAM CARSON AND PATRICK MORRIS

12. Making this Place Our Own 68
    PHILIP LITTLE AND ROBERT PARSONS

13. A Star of the Sea 76
     CAPTAIN WILLIAM JACKMAN

14. A Man of His Time 82
     SIR WILFRED THOMASON GRENFELL

15. Granite and Lilies 89
     CAPTAIN BOB BARTLETT

16. Northern Newfoundland Nurse-Midwife 96
     MYRA BENNETT

17. Birthing for Generations 104
     TRADITIONAL NEWFOUNDLAND MIDWIVES

18. A Millionaire in Seals 108
     CAPTAIN ABRAM KEAN

19. The Grand Dames of Newfoundland Politics 115
     ARMINE GOSLING, FRANCES MCNEIL,
     AND LADY HELENA SQUIRES

20. Bread and Roses 122
     ST. JOHN'S ACTIVIST JULIA SALTER EARLE

21. Rebel with a Cause 126
     PEARCE POWER

22. The Nightingale of the North 134
     MARIE TOULINGUET

23. "Calling Newfoundland" 141
     MARGOT DAVIES

24. Newfoundland Folk Renaissance 147
     RUFUS GUINCHARD. EMILE BENOIT,
     AND MINNIE WHITE

25. Comedy without Malice 155
     TED RUSSELL

26. Confederation-Bound 160
     JOSEPH ROBERTS SMALLWOOD

INTRODUCTION

Some people's rogues are other people's heroes, and vice versa. This book shines a light on a number of Newfoundlanders, some of them well known, others still obscured in the settling dust of time. They emerge from a history that has been tumultuous and sometimes dark, but always fascinating.

The island portion of our province, or nation as some call us, has been fought over by the English, Basques, and French, as well as by the Indigenous Mi'kmaq and Beothuk. Our waters have been infested by pirates. Our land has been the refuge of hideaways.

We often see ourselves as the victims of colonial forces, yet some Newfoundlanders have attained international prominence. We are often seen as less advanced than the rest of North America, yet, as some of the following stories show, we have been in the vanguard of important world developments. Some of our people have risen to great heights in the arts, northern exploration, broadcasting, and myriad other endeavours. This book uncovers some of these stories and celebrates them. It also reveals the complexity of certain famous Newfoundlanders—those who might be considered rogues.

As schoolbook history often records the influence of men and ignores the contribution of women, we have made efforts to restore gender parity. The influence of women is vital to Newfoundland's identity, and these pages tell the feminine, as well as the masculine, side of Newfoundland history.

Some of the lives in this volume reach far back to an era in which history merges with folklore. Such is the reality of Newfoundland's early history—specific facts have not always been reliably recorded in primary sources (i.e. newspapers, diaries, letters, etc). Where practical details are sketchy, we have compared sources and made choices about which of these are more likely to be accurate. We hope that the stories contained here will spark both interest and debate, showing that Newfoundland history is alive in our hearts and minds

All the characters in this volume are part of Newfoundland's pre-Confederation history, the history that is less generally known and understood. In this volume, we are especially interested in those who have helped to mold Newfoundland's national identity.

In this book, we have concentrated solely on stories from the island part of the province. Labrador has its own history—and its own rogues and heroes. Their stories will be told another time.

Paul Butler & Maura Hanrahan
St. John's, 2005

AN ACCIDENTAL DISCOVERY

JOHN CABOT

"Be it known to all, that we have given and granted to our well-beloved John Cabot, citizen of Venice...full authority...to sail to all parts, countries and seas of the East, of the West and of the North, under our banner and ensigns...to set up our banner on any new-found-land...to seek out and discover whatsoever isles...of the heathen and infidels, which before the time have been unknown to all Christians..."

John Cabot sailing from Bristol. Photo credit: The Book of Newfoundland, Vol 1.

So read King Henry VII's permission, dated March 5, 1496, for John Cabot to explore in the King's name. The consequence of the King's decision is, of course, well known to Newfoundlanders. Yet when Cabot set sail from Bristol on May 2, 1497, on his westward journey through the Atlantic, the "new-found-land" he was searching for was in fact eastern Asia. Among the exotic resources he hoped to harvest were spices and silks, not the unglamourous codfish.

So the story of Cabot has to take into account the largely accidental nature of his discoveries. This, however, is also very much in keeping with the speculative nature of his age of exploration. Christopher Columbus also believed that he had "discovered" an as yet un-colonized part of eastern Asia in 1492 when he stumbled upon the West Indies. He would in time achieve a unique kind of immortality among explorers as the discoverer of America.

John Cabot, or Giovanni Caboto, was originally from Genoa, Italy, and became a Venetian citizen in 1476. He was evidently a merchant and navigator of some standing and travelled to Mecca in Arabia where he saw the caravans transporting spices from the east. He settled in England in 1495 and had homes in the premier western port of Bristol and in Blackfriars, London. There was a powerful colony of Italian merchants and moneylenders in London at that time, and proximity to the English court and seat of government is likely to have been vital to the success of business.

In fact, John Cabot had already worked for the Crown, helping in negotiations with the king of Denmark regarding English trade with Iceland. England at that time exchanged its cloth for Icelandic fish. The need for this particular commodity from a foreign power would lessen dramatically after John Cabot's explorations.

After Columbus's voyage to America, Bristol's merchant community was abuzz with excitement over the possibilities. Just as Columbus had courted Queen Isabella and King Ferdinand of

> "[King] Henry might think he owned Newfoundland, but the Portuguese seemed to regard it as part of their overseas empire, and even Spain fancied it had a claim. Before long, France was to entertain the same notion." Patrick O'Flaherty in *Old Newfoundland*.

2

Spain, so merchants and would-be explorers now clamoured for King Henry VII's patronage.

The time was ripe for expansion. Henry VII was the first of the Tudor kings. Since his ascension at the Battle of Bosworth Field in 1485, England had begun one of its most prosperous and relatively peaceful periods in history. The King could not afford to ignore the revenues and strategic advantages that might come from expansion into foreign lands.

Cabot approached the King with his petition, in effect a licence to sail from, and back to, British ports in the King's name. In keeping with tradition, the wording was colourful and full of flattery:

> "Please it your Highnes of your most noble and abundant grace to graunt unto John Cabotto...your gracious letters patentes under your grete sele..."

Cabot had the backing of the Bristol merchants, and, in a letter, Henry gave Cabot the answer he wanted.

In reality, the deal was rather one-sided and very much in the King's favour. Although the charter granted Cabot the permission he needed, there was no financial help of any kind from the Crown when it came to acquiring ships or crew. And further, Cabot was bound by the charter to pay the King a fifth of all financial gain accruing from his voyages.

Contemporary accounts describe Cabot as being dressed in silk and being followed everywhere by the adoring English.

These conditions were in no way unusual, however. For many years after Cabot's voyage, the privateers who pledged to defend the Crown's trade and do battle with foreign vessels were required to outfit entirely at their own expense.

After one aborted attempt in 1496, Cabot set out on May 2, 1497. The crew, according to Judge D.W. Prowse, numbered seventeen, and the ship, thought to be called the *Mathew*, the *Matthew* or perhaps the *Matea* after Cabot's wife, was a small vessel of fifty tons.

On June 24, thirty-five days into the voyage, someone on board the ship sighted land. Convinced that this was China, they approached close to the coast, anchored and rowed to shore, where they raised the arms of the English King and the Pope. Although it can never be proved beyond doubt that this was Newfoundland, most commentators and historians now agree that the land Cabot and his crew stepped

On June 24, thirty-five days into the voyage, someone on board the ship sighted land.

upon that day was likely to have been Cape Bonavista on Newfoundland's northeast coast.

Cabot and his crew spent no more time on land, but returned to the ship and explored the coast for about a month. They returned home on August 6, apparently to a hero's welcome, and achieved the nickname "great admiral." Contemporary accounts describe him as dressing in silk and being followed everywhere by the adoring English. The King granted him a sum of £20.00 a year.

Whatever the misunderstandings about the land they had found, its importance to the Crown was already becoming obvious. "The king has gained a great part of Asia without a stroke of the sword..." said one contemporary account (a December 1497 letter from a London-based Italian merchant, Raimondo di Soncino, to the Duke of Milan): "...The sea is full of fish which are taken not only with the net but with a basket." The same letter continued: "...they can bring so many fish that the kingdom will have no more business with Islanda [Iceland], and that from this country there will be a

"What might have been our destiny had Columbus, not Cabot with his west of England sailors, discovered North America? Heaven only knows what would have been our fate—possibly a great Spanish possession, with chronic revolutions, disordered finances, pronunciamentos, half-breeds, and fusillades." Historian Daniel Woodley Prowse on how fortunate it was that Newfoundland became an English, rather than a Spanish, possession.

very great trade in the fish they call stock fish [cod]."

Cabot set out again on a westward journey from Bristol the following year, and from then he slips off the record of history. It is difficult to tell whether he died or merely left England. Either way, his name remains synonymous with the discovery of Newfoundland and with the first mention of Newfoundland's great resource: codfish.

PRINCE OF PIRATES

PETER EASTON

Photo credit: Job Photograph Collection, Maritime History Archive, Memorial University of Newfoundland.

He reigned supreme along the coastline between Ferryland and Harbour Grace between 1611 and 1614. He raided French and Spanish ships, and commandeered English fishing vessels and armaments for his own use, press-ganging fishermen into his own service. While using Newfoundland as his base, he undertook raids so daring in tropical waters they would soon become the stuff of legend. All this without the slightest authority from the Crown.

And yet Peter Easton did not see himself as a rogue or pirate. He lived in an era when the dividing line between traitor and patriot was very thin indeed, and political change could cause someone to fall out of favour or come into grace overnight. And his confidence was well founded. He was born a gentleman and would die with an aristocratic title. As though in defiance of the Crown, which in his eyes failed to give him the legal authority he was clearly due, he flew the St. George's Cross from his flagship's (the *Happy Adventure*) mast.

He had the arrogance of a man who had descended from a proud lineage. His ancestors served in the Crusades and, much later, the Eastons distinguished themselves against the Spanish Armada. When he first came to the waters off Newfoundland in 1602, Easton was a loyal Crown servant commanding a convoy to protect the Newfoundland fishing fleet. As a privateer with a commission from Queen Elizabeth I, he carried out the duties required of him, protecting the English fishery in Newfoundland. This was rough and dangerous work, and the authority given him by the Crown gave him a very wide leeway. He could requisition arms from English fishing vessels if necessary. At this time, fishing ships always carried a few small cannons to protect the valuable cargo of fish from pirates and foreign vessels. Easton could also take supplies and legally press-gang fishermen into service for him. And it went without saying he could attack the ships and wharves of the enemy as much as he wished, particularly the hated Spanish.

Privateers were generally wealthy men who accepted such commissions from the Crown and purchased their own ships to carry out their duties. They were highly adventurous characters who had chosen a life of danger and adventure when they might just as easily have languished in wealth and indolence at home.

Peter Easton dressed in the highest fashions—silver-buckled shoes, lace cuffs and silk stockings—and entertained in some style aboard his flagship, the *Happy Adventure*.

The turning point in Easton's career came in 1603 when Elizabeth I was succeeded by James I. The new King sued for peace with Spain and cancelled all letters of commission to privateers. This effectively rendered Easton and many more of his occupation unemployed. Easton took the step common with many in his position and simply carried on the same activities as though nothing had changed. In doing so, however, he crossed the thin line between protector on the high seas and lawless pirate. It must have seemed something of a technicality out in the wild waters, and in reality it made little difference in day-to-day life. He continued attacking Spanish ships for gold in the West Indies and the Mediterranean. Closer to home he carried on levying protection money from English ships. In 1610, he blockaded the Bristol Channel, effectively controlling the shipping entering and leaving the powerful western English ports.

Like many pirates, Easton was in fact acting on behalf of a very powerful protector. The family of Killigrews from Falmouth, Cornwall, was his patron and agent. This family supplied and financed Easton's expeditions and took a share in his profits. Easton's fleet was one of several under the protection of the Killigrews family, and a safe haven was provided for such ships along Cornwall's rugged coasts.

The Killigrews family were not outlaws. They were involved

The turning point in Easton's career came in 1603 when Elizabeth I was succeeded by James I. The new King sued for peace with Spain and cancelled all letters of commission to privateers.

in court politics on a high level, representing a potent and influential faction in the English court. Members of the Killigrews family even acted in an advisory capacity to the King.

And this vital connection at court allowed the Killigrews to tip Easton off regarding the most serious threat to his pirating career so far. In 1611, the King had sent an envoy to seize and arrest Easton. Ironically, the King's agent on this occasion was Henry Mainwarring, a privateer who, like Easton, would later turn pirate.

To escape this threat, Easton sailed first south along the west coast of Africa and then to Newfoundland. When he arrived with ten well-armed ships in St. John's harbour, he invited Sir Richard Whitbourne, fishing admiral of the port of St. John's, on board his flagship. Whitbourne must have had serious qualms about boarding the gentleman-pirate's vessel, although he knew the reality of politics in the colonies was far from black and white.

As it happened, Easton entertained Whitbourne lavishly in his well-appointed cabin and continued to entertain him for eleven weeks as a virtual prisoner until Whitbourne, who ironically held a Vice-Admiralty commission for the suppression of piracy, agreed to plead Easton's case with the Crown for a royal pardon.

> **When he arrived with ten well-armed ships in St. John's harbour, he invited Sir Richard Whitbourne, fishing admiral of the port of St. John's, on board his flagship.**

As it was, James I was by now only too happy to grant Easton a pardon, so far had rumours of his great wealth begun to spread. It was at this time common practice for pardons to be bought from the Crown. At least three applications for pardons were made by Easton, including the one through Whitbourne. At least two were bestowed by the King in February and in November 1612. But such was the unpredictability of early seventeenth century travel and the life of a pirate that none of the pardons appear to have reached Easton.

While in Newfoundland, Easton is estimated to have taken as many as 1,500 fishermen for his ships. Some may have been volunteers, but the majority were undoubtedly taken by force. One hundred and eighty men crammed into each ship with the crew sleeping between decks in great human clumps—billets in stark contrast to Easton's own spacious cabin with rugs, ornaments and bookcases. And yet, by all accounts, his "crew" held their leader in high esteem. Easton's relationship with the great early merchants and colonizers was patchy, but pragmatic concerns usually kept a certain "live-and-let-live" balance.

By arrangement, Easton left John Guy's colony at Cuper's Cove (now Cupids) alone and even protected Guy's supply of salt for the preservation of fish. He did not, however, allow Guy to become too powerful, and prevented him from establishing another colony in Renews.

But even as he wielded power over Conception Bay, Easton was not content to settle in one place. While retaining his main Newfoundland fortress in Harbour Grace and a secondary base in Ferryland, Easton went south to the Caribbean to prey on Spanish shipping. On one occasion, he captured an English ship which he caught trading slaves with Spaniards off the coast of Guinea in Africa. He brought it all the way back to Newfoundland, but Whitbourne persuaded him to return it to its owner.

Easton had some spectacular successes. One of these was a raid on the reputedly unassailable fort of Moro Castle, Puerto Rico, which had once withstood a siege by Sir Francis Drake. Easton successfully made off with stockpiles of Spanish gold and brought it home to Harbour Grace along with a Spanish ship, the *San Sebastian*, which was also full of treasure.

On returning he found that Harbour Grace had been captured by French Basques. He succeeded in recapturing the town and sinking the Basque ships. The forty-seven men lost in the battle were buried at Bear Cove, just north of Harbour Grace, now known as the pirate's graveyard.

The most daring attack of all was still to come, however. In 1614, Easton hatched a scheme to intercept the Spanish Plate Fleet. This was the annual run of all the gold and other riches extracted from Central America. The haul was taken on a tortuous overland and sea route first to the West Indies before it was shipped to the centre of the empire in Spain. Easton ambushed the Spanish fleet in the Azores, a group of islands in the Atlantic Ocean. He arrived off the Barbary Coast with Spain's entire annual Caribbean revenue. He was taken in by a Tunisian prince and entertained as a hero.

A year later, Easton, who was by now eager to retire, found a home in Villefranche on the Riviera, a free port for pirates. He was welcomed by the Duke of Savoy who had heard rumours of the pirate's great wealth, which is said to have been two million pounds sterling, an almost unimaginable sum in 1615. There Easton bought a palace, married a woman of noble blood, and acquired the title Marquis of Savoy.

CARBONEAR'S ELUSIVE PRINCESS

SHEILA NAGUEIRA

Carbonear from Saddle Hill, probably pre-1930.
Photo credit: Centre for Newfoundland Studies,
Memorial University of Newfoundland.

Reclaiming facts from the web of folklore is seldom an easy task. The legend of Sheila NaGueira, the "Irish Princess," said to be the first European woman to give birth in Newfoundland (after the Vikings), is particularly rich with colourful yet conflicting details.

Sheila is variously known as the island's first schoolteacher, a midwife, a herbal doctor and, according to some accounts, a fearless defender of her Carbonear home against both unfriendly natives and the French. Many of these images come to us through the four-hundred-year fabric of oral history. They are supplemented by historical research, some adventure fiction, and reinforced by the literature of a thriving tourism industry.

The version of the story most often repeated is the one found in the *Encyclopedia of Newfoundland and Labrador*. The details are these: In 1602, Sheila was a young Irish noblewoman sailing from France, where she had been studying in a French convent run by her aunt, an abbess. Taken prisoner in the English Channel by a Dutch privateer, she was rescued by Peter Easton, an English privateer loyal to Queen Elizabeth I. Easton's fleet was on its way to Newfoundland to protect the English fishing fleet there, and took its rescued prisoners to the New World. En route, Sheila fell in love with Gilbert Pike, one of Easton's lieutenants, and they were married. Pike left Easton's employ, and he and Sheila became "planters," small business owners in the fishery, in a place called Mosquito (now Bristol's Hope) on Newfoundland's Avalon Peninsula. They moved to nearby Carbonear Island in 1611 to escape the return of Easton who, under the reign of James I, had lapsed into piracy. When Easton's pirates left Newfoundland in 1613–14, Sheila and Gilbert returned to the area near Mosquito, which later became known as Carbonear.

NaGueira (Nageira, or NaGeira), according to this version, was an epithet meaning "the beautiful." Sheila was actually an O'Connor, the daughter of a claimant to the Irish throne of Connaught, hence the nickname "The Irish Princess."

Over the years, however, original documentation and records have stubbornly refused to confirm any of the facts. Those who try to verify Sheila and Gilbert's existence have taken comfort from a census in 1681 which mentions a Pike in Carbonear with no children, ten employees and two boats, a fragment of factual evidence that at least confirms the early presence of a Pike family in a social position similar to that which Gilbert and Sheila would have found themselves had they indeed landed in Mosquito in 1602–3 as planters.

The thinness of the historical record has created a reliance on oral history, which in turn gives rise to some unique problems of its own. Versions of Sheila's story are manifold and contradictory. One account has

> That she should be known as "the beautiful," just as William was known as "the Conqueror" ...echoed a royal tradition and...reinforced the theory that she was indeed a princess.

Sheila leading the battle for Carbonear against the French in 1697, almost a century after her supposed landing in Newfoundland. So disparate are these oral accounts that there were at one time some serious claims made that an ancient weathered gravestone with the only legible date reading 1753 marked Sheila's burial place. The controversy continued until 1982, when the Canadian Conservation Institute confirmed that, although a Pike (John) was buried there, the crumbling stone made no mention of a Sheila.

It's easy to see why the various legends of Sheila should have taken on a life so far beyond the confines of plausibility. The date most quoted for her landing (1602–3) is highly significant. The first official record of a European baby born in Newfoundland was on March 27, 1613 to a Mr. and Mrs. Guy (or possibly Gore). If Gilbert and Sheila had children, as they are reputed to have done, the event was likely to have preceded this, and they would have been Newfoundland's first family of European descent; so Sheila would have been the mother of the new nation of Newfoundland. It is no wonder, perhaps, that Carbonear lore should have her as a kind of New World Joan of Arc, fighting foreign invaders, and performing minor miracles in healing the sick with herbal remedies. Perhaps the Irishwoman who left Europe behind in the dying days of Elizabeth I's reign replaced the Virgin Queen in the hearts of the partly English population of succeeding generations. Perhaps she became, like Queen Bess, a mythical icon and a figurehead of the oldest religion in the world—goddess worship.

But what remains a curiosity are the number of fairly precise details that have been incorporated into the legend. The twentieth century saw many writers contributing to the story, clarifying and systematizing the existing myths of Carbonear. The first of these seems to be a local historian, William Munn. Much later on, Harold Horwood, notably in his *Pirates and Outlaws of Canada* (1984), made efforts to take the tale and embed it into known history. It was Horwood who first argued, from largely undisclosed research, that Sheila was the O'Connor of the royal line and the name "NaGeira" meant "the beautiful." That she should be known as "the beautiful," just as William was known as "the Conqueror" and Edward "the Confessor," echoed a royal tradition and, for Horwood, reinforced the theory that she was indeed a princess.

> If Gilbert and Sheila had children, as they are reputed to have done...they would have been Newfoundland's first family of European descent; so Sheila would have been the mother of the new nation of Newfoundland.

While Horwood researched and argued historical likelihoods, it was the popular Newfoundland "pirate story" writer P.J. Wakeham who, deriving his information from the oral histories of the Pikes in the area, is more responsible than anyone for popularizing the tale. His novel *The Legend of Princess Sheila*, first published in 1958, has Sheila as the stoical leader, guiding and teaching her people and acting as a general in Carbonear's resistance to the great French Canadian naval captain Pierre Le Moyne d'Iberville in 1697.

Wakeham, who billed himself strictly as a popular writer and not a scholar, later deferred to Horwood's theory over Sheila's name. In a 1987 reprint he changed Sheila's name to O'Connor.

But Horwood's theory about the name, although making it into the *Encyclopedia of Newfoundland and Labrador*, is far from watertight. A hundred years ago, the Pikes of Carbonear referred to the legendary Sheila not as NaGueira, but as *MaGella*. A baby named after Sheila born in 1917 was given her name, which was by then spelt *MaGeila*.

It appears to have been Newfoundland museum curator Leo English who (in the *Newfoundland Quarterly* of June 1949) decisively fixed Sheila's surname as NaGeira by whimsically identifying her with the popular song by the Irish poet Thomas Moore (1779–1852). For Moore, the name *Sheila NaGeira* was likely to have been entirely symbolic, as Sheila was an affectionate term for Ireland. So the name literally meant "Ireland, the beautiful."

Whether a story is true or not is far less important than how it came into being. Even people who search for historical evidence of Sheila can gain comfort from the fact that, while it seems impossible to verify her existence, the fog of Newfoundland's early history makes it equally difficult to rule out any theory entirely. Far from dying away, recent decades have added new layers of possibility to the story. In the 1980s, at least one folklorist from University College Dublin was excited about the identity of Carbonear's Irish

---

Sheila's legend looms larger than ever in Newfoundland today.

A quote from the *2003 Travel Guide*, published by the Government of Newfoundland and Labrador: "An Irish princess [Princess Sheila] captured by pirate Peter Easton settled near here with one of Easton's crew, Gilbert Pike, and lived happily ever after."

Travellers to Newfoundland will also find: a NaGeira House Inn, Carbonear; and The NaGeira Theatre Festival, Carbonear (mid-July to late August annually).

Princess. He argued that an Irish political song from the late 1600s called "Sile Ni Ghadra" (a Gaelic name which can be Anglicized to Sheila NaGeira) could well have come from Sheila's own story, and that she was famous not only in Newfoundland but also in Ireland.

What is certain is that Newfoundland's Sheila Na-Gueira is a character enduring enough to weather all the historical deconstruction thrown at her and remain a formidable, if elusive, figure in Newfoundland culture.

There is a goddess from Ireland called Sheila Na Gig, whose face and figure are carved into ancient rocks and used as church "gargoyles." She is always depicted as a very old, haglike woman, and seems to represent passion, birth, sex and death. As stories of Sheila NaGueira often state that the "Irish Princess" lived to a great age, it is likely that, through the years, memories of this well-known Irish goddess have contributed to Sheila NaGueira's legend.

LADY SARA KIRKE

Ferryland. Photo credit: Centre for Newfoundland Studies, Memorial University of Newfoundland.

Sara Kirke lived in an age of contradictions. In Stuart England, the land of her birth, women, in many ways, counted for little. They were considered to be men's inferior in every way: physically, intellectually, and even spiritually. The class system was rigid and extended to gender and race; women, like non-whites, were not the equal of the white man. On the other hand, Sara was born into aristocratic circles where women had some purchase. They were taught to read, and some, like Sara, could even write. They participated in family enterprises; they had to, for their men were often away doing the business of King and country or expanding their own empires. In this way, upper-class women like Sara were encouraged to develop their own skills and independence.

The downside was that women's contribution was not recognized in law or anywhere else. They were legally considered to be their husband's property. The saving grace for many women was "dower rights," through which a widow got one-third of her husband's estate, safe even from his creditors.

Sara would benefit from dower rights. This and her own hard work and sharp eye for business made her into one of North America's earliest and most successful entrepreneurs. Her domain was the Pool Plantation at Ferryland, about halfway down what is now known as the Southern Shore. With her husband, she lived on a narrow, grassy promontory that stretched hundreds of yards into the western North Atlantic. The plantation was the greatest hub of activity on the entire island of Newfoundland in the 1600s, and for much of that time, from 1651 until 1679, Lady Sara ran it.

Her husband, Sir David Kirke, was an ambitious, formidable man whose part in Canadian history is frequently underestimated. With his brothers, he captured Quebec and Nova Scotia for the English in 1628 and later became governor of Newfoundland. In 1637, with the Marquis of Hamilton and the Earls of Pembroke and Holland, he was made co-proprietor of Newfoundland. (Lord Baltimore had lost his rights over the place when he deserted.) Once ensconced in the mansion house at Ferryland with his wife Lady Sara, Kirke encouraged British settlement in Newfoundland, collected a five per cent tax on all fish and oil taken by foreign fishermen, and fortified the choice spots of Ferryland, St. John's, and Bay de Verde, Conception Bay.

> **In return for capturing Nova Scotia and Quebec for the English in 1628, Sir David Kirke was granted a Coat of Arms. His Arms were forgotten for a long time, but were rediscovered and were adopted as the official Coat of Arms for Newfoundland in the 1920s.**

Kirke was on the side of the monarchy, and so it was inevitable he would run afoul of the revolutionary Oliver Cromwell, who had come to power back in England. Cromwell feared Kirke would use Newfoundland to stage a counter-revolution and bring the King back to the throne. He recalled Kirke to England and accused him of not paying taxes he had collected in the name of the government, although the charges were never substantiated. Lady Sara came to England with her husband, but returned to Newfoundland while things were still unresolved, presumably to make sure the Pool Plantation kept running. Perhaps she was secretly pleased that Cromwell, who was keeping her husband on a short leash, allowed her to cross the Atlantic. Then she got bad news from England; Kirke was thrown in jail as a result of a suit brought by Lord Baltimore's heir. He died there in 1654.

Lady Sara was now a widow in Newfoundland. She had dower rights, but she also had a debt of £60,000, a large sum of money now, but vast in those days. She could remarry and start over, well shot of Kirke and his debts, but she had no peers in Ferryland and probably none in Newfoundland. There was no question of her marrying beneath herself in those days. She could return to England and remarry; there were aristocratic men aplenty there. She could live with her own affluent family in the Old Country if she wished.

Her other option was to stay in Ferryland and make a go of it; although it appeared to be the most difficult one available, this is the option she chose. She may have been following her mother-in-law's example. Like Sara, Elizabeth Kirke spent much of her married life running the family business while her husband was away. After her husband died, Elizabeth was a successful wine merchant in London.

Memorial University business professor Robert Sexty is one of the few people to have studied Lady Sara Kirke's life. He writes: "Little substantial documentation exists about Lady Sara Kirke, but what can be pieced together indicates a woman of strong character and great resourcefulness."

Indeed so! According to the 1660 Census, she was the largest planter in Newfoundland. Ten years later, she was still the largest planter. She owned more stages, boats, and train (cod liver oil) vats than any other planter. She also employed more servants. She did business with English merchants as well as merchants

"Although it appeared to be the most difficult course available to her, this is the option she chose."

from Spain. Lady Sara even managed to survive and salvage her enterprises when the Dutch raided and burned the Ferryland colony, including her premises, in 1663.

In 1675, she was still in business. Only five per cent of the planters at the Pool Plantation owned five boats; Lady Sara, long after she'd been widowed, was the only boat-owning woman among them. These planters had an average of 25.7 servants; Sara had twenty-five men working for her. Her sons George, David and Phillip were also planters. Of them, only Phillip had a going concern to rival that of his mother that particular year. The next year, Lady Sara was responsible for more boats than her sons David and George combined, although she didn't employ as many men as either of them.

As did her sons, she ran her enterprises without the support of the Crown. Charles II was restored to the throne in 1660, putting the status of the colony at Ferryland up in the air. Lady Sara petitioned him with a sugary letter, typical of those written to the monarch during the era, asking him to grant power over the colony to her eldest son, George. She was not successful, for the King gave it instead to Cecil Calvert, the second Lord Baltimore. Fortunately, Calvert never bothered to claim control of the colony for himself, and Lady Sara was able to soldier on.

In their study of Lady Sara, Robert Sexty and Sue Sexty conclude: "Lady Sara appears to have been motivated by necessity, a desire to be independent, and a wish to control her own future and financial destiny." In this, she was perhaps not atypical of the men and women who came to Newfoundland from the shores of England, Ireland, and elsewhere in Europe. Her status as a woman and an aristocrat gave her a unique set of circumstances, which she managed to work to her advantage to become the most successful merchant on the English Shore.

Lady Sara is believed to have died in the early 1680s and lies buried on the grassy Ferryland Downs, overlooking the sea. Her sons survived her and carried on their successful enterprises at Ferryland and elsewhere on the Avalon Peninsula until 1696, when the French raid destroyed them. The Kirke men were captured and imprisoned at Placentia. Two of the brothers died there, while the third died soon after at St. John's.

LADY SARA'S WORLD

Colony: A seventeenth century English settlement in Newfoundland authorized by Royal charter.

English Shore: From Bonavista to Trepassey.

Plantation: Houses, structures, and ground adjacent to the foreshore of a cove, bay or harbour.

Planter: An early settler in Newfoundland (as opposed to a migratory fisherman). It also means, especially in the context of Lady Sara Kirke, the owner of fishing premises and boats.

Proprietorship: Ownership of a territory granted by the Crown to an individual or group in whom all governing rights were vested.

Servant: Man or woman indentured or engaged on wages or shares in the fishery.

PETER KERRIVAN AND THE MASTERLESS MEN

Photo credit: Job Photograph Collection, Maritime History Archive, Memorial University of Newfoundland.

The legend of The Masterless Men remains an elusive and romantic episode in the late eighteenth century history of the island. It is the true story of a small group of men who in the 1700s defied the British Navy, the Crown and the fishing masters and, under threat of execution if caught, lived as outlaws on the wild lands of the Avalon Peninsula.

Like Robin Hood, the tale of the Masterless Men epitomizes the rebellious spirit of the people and the injustice from which they were forced to flee. Unlike Robin Hood, this story is true in its bare essentials and has been verified by both the military records and the oral history of the Southern Shore.

Newfoundland settlement around 1750 was characterized by indentured servitude. The British Navy also backed up the authority of the fishing masters whose contracted workers were in many ways only a small step up from slaves. In fact, many of the young Irish men brought by merchant skippers to the Southern Shore were quite literally sold to fishing masters. Their price was £50 a head. This practice of selling fishery workers, apprentices or "youngsters" as they were known, was challenged by the British authorities who felt that all profits should go to the Crown. A £10 fine was imposed on merchant skippers for each articled crew member left behind in Newfoundland at the end of the season. But a large profit margin still remained, and the trade continued. According to Harold Horwood, "the practice of selling [young Irish men] into semi-slavery survived into the nineteenth century."

Life for these fishing apprentices was characterized by constant, dangerous toil and by frequent use of corporal punishment. Even the small settlement of Ferryland boasted three whipping posts and a gibbet for hanging. Men were not free to simply leave employment. As indentured workers, they owed their fishing master a set number of years' work. Therefore, to leave a contracted position was to become an outlaw in the eyes of the Naval authorities who were there to protect the fishery and maintain their idea of law and order.

The term "masterless man" already existed to describe any man who ran away from a fishing crew to try and live independently as an outlaw. But in 1750, one very small group of desperate runaways would claim the title for themselves and live for a whole generation or more, carving out a subsistence on the Butter Pot Barrens about nine miles inland from the Southern Shore port of Ferryland.

The story begins with one Peter Kerrivan, a deserter not from a fishing settlement, but from the British Navy, which at this time was a brutal institution. Deck officers routinely carried whips or canes and meted out punishment to a half-starved crew. Flogging was common, as was being dunked from the yardarm. Even keel-hauling was yet to be outlawed. Tradition has it that Kerrivan had originally been press-ganged into the Navy.

Somehow Kerrivan escaped the Navy in 1750 when his ship was in Ferryland, and led a group of two or three indentured fishermen to the Butter Pot Barrens. They hid out from the authorities, choosing the Southern Butter Pot, a craggy stone peak, as their lookout and base.

Beginning as a desperate group trying to evade apprehension and the certain death that would follow, the Society of Masterless Men, as they would become known, began to develop survival skills. There were roughly 5,000 caribou on the Avalon Peninsula at that time, and this herd became the group's staple for both food and clothing. It is believed that the Masterless Men had contact with Newfoundland's Aboriginal people—the Mi'kmaq, who had at least a seasonal presence in the district, and also the Beothuk, whose numbers were already dwindling very dangerously. Regular communication with these groups gave these sailors and fishermen the experience they needed to defy all odds and stay alive on the barrens. Oral history also suggests that the Masterless Men traded with the Mi'kmaq and Beothuk through the years.

Word of mouth about the escapees spread and, far from dwindling, the numbers of Masterless Men started to grow with fresh runaways from the settlements along the shore.

Word of mouth about the escapees quickly spread. Far from dwindling, the numbers of Masterless Men started to grow with fresh runaways from the settlements along the shore. Fearing widespread desertion of their lucrative fishing industry, the British authorities ordered the Navy to track down and make an example of the Masterless Men with a mass execution. But it was several years before the first serious expedition was mounted by a Naval Lieutenant and a party of marines.

By this time, Kerrivan and his men had become not only skilled hunters but expert all-around woodsmen. They had learned to move swiftly across the barrens using the many interconnecting lakes. They also had a private network of paths which twisted through the brush.

The Masterless Men had been warned in advance of the planned move against them and had set up a series of cunning blind trails which were well cut and marked, suggesting constant use. But these paths only led into bogs or impenetrable thickets.

The naval party were held up in this maze, and it took them some time to find Kerrivan's hideout. Eventually, however, they did find the log cabins of the outlaws at a spot very close to their lookout on the Southern Butter Pot. But when the marines closed in, they discovered the place to be deserted. All trace of life and all supplies were long gone. Kerrivan and his men had taken advantage of their confusion and had moved off toward the west and north, into the area now called the Avalon Wilderness Area. The Navy burned the cabins and went back to base claiming that at least they had cleared the outlaws away from the area and destroyed their homes.

But, of course, the Masterless Men returned. During the years that followed, the Navy burned down their cabins three times, and each time they were rebuilt. Apart from their expert outdoors skills, Kerrivan and his men had other aids by this time. They had begun to secretly trade with the settlements along the coast. They sold caribou meat and hides and received in turn vital supplies like flour, tea, and bullets for their hunting rifles. It is likely that their contacts tipped them off more than once when there was a plan to apprehend them.

Oral records passed down by Howard Morry of Ferryland tell about Mr. Morry's great-grandmother who, as a little girl, visited Ferryland from her home in Aquaforte. She saw the four boys hanging from the British frigate—the only Masterless Men ever caught by the Navy.

One time the Navy was successful, catching four recent young runaways who had joined the Masterless Men. They were tried in a quick court martial upon the deck of an English frigate in Ferryland. The young men were hanged by the yardarm of the same ship. They remained there swinging, an example to all who passed the community.

It is easy to sympathize with the noble outlaw and turn him into a folk hero, particularly when all these men were indeed the subjects of such severe injustice. But there is some evidence to suggest that the Masterless Men were not entirely benign. In 1789, for instance, a petition from Ferryland was sent to the governor requesting military aid against bands of outlaws. It seems very likely that these men were descendants of Kerrivan's original runaways. In the same year as the petition, four men gave themselves up to authorities on condition that their only punishment would be deportation to Ireland.

Such a deal illustrates the gradual relaxation in the laws during the turn of the eighteenth century. Because the rules of indentured servitude were becoming less strict, the ranks of the Masterless Men began to dwindle. It was becoming more possible for fishery workers to move away from fishing masters. It is believed that many of the Masterless Men themselves settled down in some of the more remote and inaccessible parts of Newfoundland's coast where they might escape apprehension for previous crimes. Some of the Masterless Men had already taken wives from the settlements and possibly from among the Mi'kmaq or Beothuk. Kerrivan himself is said to have had a wife, four sons and several daughters. But Kerrivan, unlike

> The tale of the Masterless Men remains a fascinating and, to some extent, still untold Newfoundland story. Although the subject remains elusive as non-fiction, Newfoundland writer Eldon Drodge published *Kerrivan* in 2001 (Jesperson), dramatizing the story.

some of his followers, continued to live on the Butter Pot Barrens. According to Harold Horwood, he lived to "a ripe old age as the patrician of his outlaw band, a venerable old man of the mountains."

One legacy of the Masterless Men was soon to be discovered by authorities. This was their amazing ability to carve out paths which would sometimes stretch from one part of the Avalon Peninsula to another. One route went all the way from Butter Pot Barrens to Trinity Bay. Indeed, the Masterless Men were responsible for Newfoundland's first roads. These were used gratefully many years later by the early government mail carriers.

RICHARD BROTHERS

Photo credit: *Encyclopedia of Newfoundland and Labrador, Vol. 1.*

Newfoundland-born and raised, Richard Brothers became one of the world's most outrageous self-styled prophets. He claimed not only a stature similar to that of Moses and a unique relationship with God, but also a worldly influence that would allow him to gather the lost tribes of Israel from parts of Europe and lead them home to Jerusalem.

What distinguishes Brothers from the ranks of history's deluded would-be prophets is that so many people believed him genuine, including, it was rumoured, King George III's granddaughter, the young Victoria, later to become Queen. Not only was Brothers Newfoundland's most internationally known religious zealot, his publications and prophecies also made him the most prolific and best-selling Newfoundland author in history.

Born on Christmas Day in 1757 in Admiral's Cove on the Southern Shore, Brothers was involved at an early age with the Newfoundland fishery. His father had been a military man in Placentia with the British forces, but had retired and settled with his large family, intending to live off the sea.

It is not known precisely why, but alone of his family, Richard left Newfoundland at age ten or eleven to be educated back in England. He was schooled there in Woolwich, and at fourteen years of age joined the British Navy as midshipman on board the HMS *Ocean*. In a successful career, he served in the West Indies and was promoted in time to the rank of lieutenant. He was honourably discharged on July 28, 1783, from which time he was entitled to receive a pension (or "half pay") of £54 a year.

Not quite ready to settle down, Brothers entered the merchant marines and travelled Europe for a few more years. In 1786, he married Elizabeth Hassall, but, bizarrely, never lived with her. He went straight back to his ship and continued wandering. He returned years later to find his wife living with another man, with whom she had several children.

In 1787, Brothers settled in London to live on his half-pay. During the following two years, he showed an interest in religion, attending a Baptist chapel in the Adelphi in the city. In 1789 came the first evidence that Brothers was developing some unusually strong views. In that year, he refused to take the oath of allegiance to the sovereign, a ritual which allowed him to continue collecting his pension; his refusal meant his pension was cut off.

In the argument that ensued with the Admiralty, Brothers wrote to the *Public Ledger*, arguing against the oath on the grounds that it was supposed to be voluntary. He caused enough of a stir for the Admiralty to set about rewording the oath. Brothers would not compromise, however, wanting it abolished. In his mind, Brothers was already obeying a higher power; the Bible instructed men to "swear not at all." Also, it is quite possible he was being plagued by visions and delusions of grandeur. In time, he would become convinced that the King would one day abdicate in his favour.

Brothers was taken to the workhouse because, due to lack of income, he'd amassed debts of £30 to his landlady. While in the workhouse, his half pay was collected on his behalf and given to his landlady. He was released in February 1790, and he found a new residence in Soho, London.

Brothers began to experience visions he believed were divine in nature. First he was told by God that London would be destroyed. Then he found himself carried up to heaven where he was told by God that London would be spared because of his own pleading on behalf of the inhabitants. "There is no other man on Earth who could stand before Me and ask for such a thing," were the words he believed God had told him.

In May 1792, Brothers wrote to the King, the Prime Minister William Pitt and the Speaker of the House of Commons, saying he had received heavenly instructions informing him to address the House. He was, not surprisingly, turned down and refused entry. But, never easily discouraged, Brothers instead published further letters to the royal family and the government. While his message steadfastly refused to find an audience with the seat of power, it gained immediate interest among the populace.

There were indeed some eerie coincidences, at least initially. In his writings, he had foretold that the King of Sweden would meet a violent death. On March 29, 1792, Gustave III was indeed assassinated. He also foretold the death of Louis XVI of France, who faced the guillotine on January 21, 1793. (This, of course, was not such an outlandish prediction, given the bloody revolution which had already occurred in 1789.)

Again Brothers was in trouble for nonpayment of rents, this time for the larger sum of £70. He was sent to the debtors' side of Newgate prison. At the end of 1792, however, a compromise was reached in which he signed power of attorney whereby his half pay could be collected on his behalf. Still, he insisted on striking out the term "our sovereign Lord" in reference to the King.

Free once more, he set out on the road to Bristol, intending to leave England, perhaps for his native Newfoundland. But he was suddenly called back by another divine inspiration. He believed himself summoned back to London, where he should await a new revelation even more startling than the others.

He quickly came to believe that the prophecies of the Book of Revelations would shortly be fulfilled. He had the first of many visions in which the King would hand over earthly authority to him.

But his role of saviour was to go beyond the shores of Britain. He believed that his birthdate on Christmas Day was a sign, as was his name Brothers. He believed himself descended from King David, through James, the *brother* of Christ. In another vision, he was informed by God to tell the king, "I call you My nephew."

> He quickly came to believe that the prophecies of the Book of Revelations would shortly be fulfilled.

Now in a new lodging in Paddington Street, London, Brothers dedicated himself to writing his prophecies. His first work soon appeared, entitled, "A revealed knowledge of the PROPHECIES AND TIMES, Book the First."

Here the full scale and theme of Brothers' prophecies were for the first time clearly laid out. It involved the "RESTORATION OF THE HEBREWS to Jerusalem by the year 1798 under the revealed Prince and prophet RICHARD BROTHERS." The theory ran that all the races of Europe were descended from the Hebrews of Biblical times and were the Ten Lost Tribes of Israel.

The second book followed a couple of months later and included many wild and mainly inaccurate prophecies about imminent political changes. The most important of these involved Brothers himself. He predicted that on August 6, 1795, Britain's civil and church authority would be overthrown and that on November 19, 1795, he, Richard Brothers, would be revealed in London as the Prince of the Hebrews. King George III would then yield the crown to him, and the long-awaited Exodus to the Holy

> He predicted that...on November 19, 1795, he, Richard Brothers, would be revealed in London as the Prince of the Hebrews.

Land would begin. The books sold in the thousands in England, Ireland and America and were translated into other European languages.

Brothers had become enough of a threat to seriously worry the King and parliament. On March 4, 1795, two king's messengers came and arrested Brothers. He was brought before a committee of the Privy Council, accused of treason and declared insane. He was taken to an Asylum in Islington, London.

At first, Brothers' arrest did nothing to curb his popularity. Indeed, now he had the added appeal of a folk hero. There was also a suspicion that his arrest did not follow form and he was not given an adequate defence, which in turn fuelled rumours that Brothers was indeed a prophet and leader.

Nathaniel Brassey Halhed, an M.P., scholar and linguist, became Brothers' champion. He wrote two books in support of Brothers and argued in his favour with the House of Commons, questioning the process that had led to his incarceration.

But Brothers' biggest setback was about to come as the result of one of his own prophecies. November 19, 1795, came and went, and there was no sign of him being revealed to London as the

Prince of the Hebrews. His popularity waned, and former supporters like Halhed fell away from his cause.

But even while his popularity was in decline, he found new champions and supporters. John Finlayson, a prominent lawyer,

> Richard Brothers's visions were often of a starling and vivid nature. He once claimed to have met the devil himself "walking leisurely up Tottenham Court Road (in London)."

put his reputation on the line arguing for Brothers' release. In 1806, William Pitt, the Prime Minister who had orchestrated Brothers' incarceration, died, and John Finlayson started a new and finally successful campaign for his release.

That same year, Brothers was free, the charge of treason dropped. But the verdict of insanity would not be withdrawn, as the King apparently was still wary of Brothers as a political threat, even after all the time that had elapsed. Brothers' final years were spent as a guest of loyal converts. On January 25, 1824, he died in Finlayson's home.

Largely forgotten now, Brothers' popularity in Europe and North America was once so widespread that the British King and ministers considered him a serious threat to the stability of the British Empire.

A FIGHTING SPIRIT

DEMASDUIT

Portrait of Demasduit (Mary March), painted in 1819 by Lady Hamilton. Photo credit: National Archives of Canada.

In 1818, the Governor of Newfoundland issued one of many misguided calls for attempts to establish friendly relations with the Beothuks, or Red Indians, as they were known at the time.

The Beothuk were openly hostile to Europeans, and violent conflict between the two groups became common. Between 1750 and 1790, approximately thirteen settlers were killed. More than twice this number of Beothuk were killed. This number may seem small, but it is not; there were only several hundred Beothuk, or less, when Europeans first came to Newfoundland. In addition, they were now cut off from coastal areas because of European settlement, thus losing many of their food resources.

There was great awareness of the dwindling numbers of the Beothuk throughout the island, and some sympathy for them. The government in particular was concerned and wanted to establish friendly relations. Rather unwisely, the authorities offered a reward to any settlers who could bring a Red Indian to them. Another mistake was made when Governor Sir Charles Hamilton authorized John Peyton Jr. to travel to the interior to retrieve his boat and fishing gear, items some Beothuk men had stolen the previous autumn.

On March 1, 1819, Peyton and eight or nine heavily armed men went up the Exploits River and in to Red Indian Lake, the Beothuk's winter site. They reached a grouping of three wigwams, and a dozen Beothuk, who fled at the sight of them. Demasduit was one of them. Bogged down in the snow, she exposed her breasts, a nursing mother, begging for mercy. Demasduit was captured. Then, according to Peyton's account, the settlers and the Beothuk men yelled at each other for some time. They couldn't understand each other, but it must have been obvious that Nonosabasut, Demasduit's husband and the group's leader, wanted her back.

What happened next was tragic. One of the settlers stabbed Nonosabasut to death; another killed his brother. The settlers took the grief-stricken Demasduit with them, leaving the woman's

---

NONOSABASUT'S GRAVE

Guided by Sylvester Joe, a Mi'kmaq, William Epps Cormack came upon Nonosabasut's grave. It contained the following items:

- two small wooden images of a man and a woman
- a small doll
- several small model canoes
- two small models of boats
- an iron axe
- a bow and quiver of arrows at Nonosabut's side
- two fire-stones at his head
- a variety of decorated culinary utensils made of birch rind
- other items he could not identify

baby to die two days later. Now she was twenty-four years old and all alone in the world.

Later, a grand jury in St. John's absolved Peyton and his companions of Nonosabasut's murder. They concluded that, " ...(there was) no malice on the part of Peyton's party to get possession of any of (the Indians) by such violence as would occasion bloodshed."

The settlers took the grief-stricken Demasduit with them, leaving the woman's baby to die two days later. Now she was twenty-four years old and all alone in the world.

The men took Demasduit to Twillingate, where she went to live with the Church of England minister, Reverend John Leigh. He learned that she was also called Shendoreth and Waunathoake, but he renamed her Mary March, after the Blessed Virgin Mary and the month in which she was kidnapped. A typical Victorian, he was convinced her people were savages; his goal was to have her help him convert the rest of her people to Christianity and "civilization." Demasduit tried to escape from his home at least twice.

Through Leigh, Captain Hercules Robinson of the British ship *Favourite* met Demasduit. He wrote of her in the *Mirror* in 1820: "(She was) tall and rather stout, having small and delicate limbs, particularly her arms. Her hands and feet were very small and beautifully formed and of these she was very proud, her complexion a light copper colour, became nearly as fair as a European's after a course of washing and absence of smoke, her hair was black, which she delighted to comb and oil, her eyes larger and more intelligent than those of an Esquimaux, her teeth, small, white and regular, her cheekbones rather high, but her countenance had a mild and pleasing expression... her voice was remarkably sweet, low and musical."

Demasduit ate sparingly and disliked wine and spirits. She loved sleep; she didn't rise before nine o'clock and would take naps during the day. It is possible, of course, that this was a manifestation of fatigue brought on by ill health or perhaps by the trauma and grief she had endured. She was a good mimic and learned English easily and quickly. She explained that sixteen people lived in her wigwam. In the manner of people who have known hard times, she would hoard things. One time, some blue material went missing, and sixteen pairs of blue moccasins were found in Demasduit's trunk. Evidently, she must have still hoped to go back home. She spent much of the spring of 1819 in St. John's, brought there by Leigh and John Peyton Jr., to whom she had grown quite attached, perhaps as in the manner that kidnapped people often become attached to their captors. By June 3, Demasduit was back in Twillingate.

Between June 18 and July 14, on the Governor's order, there were several attempts, though unsuccessful, to return Demasduit to her people. Once again, friendly

If the Beothuk were alive today, what would they be doing?

- pursuing a land claim?
- attempting redress for the omission of Aboriginal people from the Terms of Union between Newfoundland and Canada?
- pressing to be registered as status Indians under the Indian Act?
- lobbying to have their communities turned into reserves?

Would they have tried to prevent or delay:

- the construction of the Newfoundland Railway?
- mining at Buchans?
- hydroelectric development in Bay d'Espoir?
- logging throughout the island?
- the construction of the Trans-Canada Highway?

They might have taken these actions in co-operation with the Mi'kmaq, with whom they had kinship and other ties.

relations were to be established with the Beothuk, if possible. Plans were made for Captain David Buchan to go overland to Red Indian Lake with Demasduit in November, the people of St. John's and Notre Dame Bay having raised the money to return the Beothuk woman to her home. But Demasduit died of tuberculosis on board Buchan's vessel, the *Grasshopper*, at Ship Cove near Botwood on January 8, 1820. The foreign disease had carried away so many of her people.

Buchan, Peyton, fifty marines, and some trappers took Demasduit's body to Red Indian Lake, but they found no Beothuk there, only signs that they had been there recently. Shanawdithit later explained that the Beothuk had watched them from the woods. They then buried Demasduit with her husband. There were only thirty-one Beothuk left then, and, not surprisingly, they were devastated. With their leader murdered, their morale was at an all-time low. Now, here was his kidnapped wife being returned to them dead by dozens of these armed men, of whom they were quite terrified. The European men left gifts—dresses, moccasins, trinkets—with Demasduit's body, but it was too little too late.

THE LAST OF THE BEOTHUK?

SHANAWDITHIT

Photo credit: National Archives of Canada.

Shanawdithit is well known to Newfoundlanders. In 1851, the *Newfoundlander* called her "a princess of Terra Nova," and not much has changed; Newfoundlanders write songs and build statues in her honour.

In 1999, *Telegram* readers voted her the most notable Aboriginal person of the past 1,000 years in the paper's Newfoundlander of the Millennium contest. She got 545 votes (57% of the total), followed by former Innu Nation president Katie Riche, who got 176, and Labrador Metis artist and *Them Days* editor Doris Saunders, with ninety-six votes[1]. Widely known as the last of her people, Shanawdithit ceased being a real person a long time ago—she became a symbol.

---

1 Interestingly, the *Telegram*'s panel of experts named Innu elder Pien Penashue the most notable Aboriginal person of the millennium.

Shanawdithit was born around 1800, during the last days of the Beothuk. At the time of her birth, there were about 200 Beothuk left. In the spring of 1823, her father died when he fell through the ice running away from a group of settlers. He left the three women in his family hungry. Shanawdithit, her mother, and her sister felt they had no choice but to go to the nearest settler, a trapper named William Cull, and beg for mercy.

They left behind a dying people; their small group now consisted of only five men, four women and three children. They were all sickly. Their decline had been rapid but sadly inevitable; in 1811, there had been only seventy-two Beothuk.

The women were taken to St. John's and then back to Exploits. Once again, naive government officials hoped that friendly relations could be established between the two groups—they seemed to have had no idea how dire the situation of the Indigenous people had become. Nor did they grasp the fact that the Beothuk were likely to resent the settlers and their government for such things as the murder of Nonosabasut and the kidnapping and subsequent death of Demasduit.

Shanawdithit's mother and sister died of tuberculosis. Renamed Nancy, Shanawdithit lived for five years with the Peytons, John Jr. and his wife, Eleanor. Bishop Inglis, the Church of England Bishop of Newfoundland and Nova Scotia, visited the family in 1827 and met Shanawdithit. He "greatly lamented" that she had learned insufficient English to be baptized and confirmed. He also mentioned that she occasionally disappeared in the woods for twenty-four hours or more at a time; this was often preceded by a sullen or anxious mood. She was fond of the Peyton children who, Inglis said, would leave their mother and go to her. He wrote, "She is ...very interesting, rather graceful, and of a good disposition, her countenance mild and her voice soft and harmonious.... She is fearful that her race has died for want of food."

Shanawdithit was returned to St. John's in 1828, where she worked as a servant. She also lived with Cormack for six weeks, who in that time recorded much of what she told him about her people. He also collected her drawings: of winter wigwams (*mamateeks*); caribou smokehouses; animals; and people. She spent the last nine months of her life at the home of Newfoundland's Attorney General Simms. During that time, she was cared for by William Carson, a medical practitioner (though not a qualified physician), who would also perform her autopsy.

When she died, her skull was presented to the Royal College of Physicians in London for study. In 1938, they turned it over to the Royal College of Surgeons. Subsequently it was destroyed during the Blitz. The whereabouts of Shanawdithit's other remains are

---

THE LONG-FORGOTTEN BUSH-BORNS

The first settlers adopted an Aboriginal lifestyle based on moving from winter residences to summer stations. They didn't bring this lifestyle from their home countries in Europe, but instead learned it from the Beothuk and Mi'kmaq of Newfoundland. For a long time, European women did not come to Newfoundland. So some intermarried with the Beothuk and Mi'kmaq and mixed Aboriginal groups.

By the mid-1700s, the British were calling Newfoundlanders "bush-borns" and "copper colours." When the anti-settlement laws relaxed in the early 1800s, the bush-borns moved out to the coast to live more openly, but their Aboriginal ancestry was quickly forgotten about.

The bush-borns flew their own flag, though, and called themselves "natives" (see the story of Robert Parsons). The flag consisted of a green spruce tree on a background of reddish-pink ochre. According to some sources, with Bishop Fleming's input—or interference—it was later transformed into the pink, white and green, recalling his native Ireland.

unknown. An investigation by the City of St. John's in the area in which they were presumed to be did not recover them. Shanawdithit had been buried in an old graveyard on the south side of the city, as recorded in the Church of England Cathedral Parish Registrar in St. John's. The graveyard was dismantled for railway construction in 1903. There was a monument on the site which reads: "This monument marks the site of the Parish Church of St. Mary the Virgin during the period 1859–1963. Fishermen and sailors from many ports found a spiritual haven within its hallowed walls. Near this spot is the burying place of Nancy Shanawdithit, very probably the last of the Beothuks who died on June 6, 1829."

> Inglis wrote, "She is ...very interesting, rather graceful, and of a good disposition, her countenance mild and her voice soft and harmonious.... She is fearful that race has died for want of food."

SOUTH COAST HEROINE

ANN HARVEY

Coast Guard vessel *Ann Harvey*. Photo credit: Canadian Coast Guard.

On a June morning in 1828, seventeen-year-old Ann Harvey and her father George went, as usual, to haul their nets. What happened next would etch Ann forever in Newfoundland history.

The Harveys lived, along with one or two other families, on a small, bare, rocky island near Isle aux Morts, or Dead Islands, as it was called then. George had come to Newfoundland from Jersey some years before, married, and with his wife had eight children, of whom Ann was the oldest. That morning, when he and Ann sighted a keg and a straw bed floating in the turbulent seas, they immediately realized a ship had been wrecked nearby.

George and Ann fetched twelve-year-old Tom, George's oldest son, and their Newfoundland dog, Hairy Man, and launched their punt with little regard for their own safety. On a nearby beach they found six men who had survived the wreck. The men told them that they were from the *Despatch,* a brig partly owned by William Lancaster of Workington, England. She had sailed from Derry, Ireland on May 29, en route to Quebec with a crew of eleven and 200 passengers. These people were almost all Irish emigrants, landless tenant farmers hoping to escape the poverty they had known all their lives. As she readied to enter the Cabot Strait, the *Despatch* suddenly hove almost on top of a large rock that rose out of the ocean.

Ann and her father took four of the men aboard their own boat and headed into the open ocean looking for more survivors. They found a large number of them on a tiny island that would thereafter be known as Wreck Rock. Archdeacon Wix, a missionary for the Society for the Propagation of the Gospel, heard the story firsthand from Ann and George. He wrote: "On a rock, three miles from their residence and one mile from shore, they discovered such of the passengers as were not drowned (thirty had died, some from exhaustion and some washed away) clinging together, as they described it, like seabirds, the rock being large enough to hold them. They had got to this small island-rock by means of a mast. This they had cut away from the vessel and made of it a bridge. By this way they passed from the vessel to the rock, George Harvie [sic] could not get nearer than about 100 of them on account of the heavy sea. He threw them a billet of wood, therefore, which the water floated toward. To this the poor wretches attached a rope. He then desired his Newfoundland dog to swim for it. By this rope the passengers who fastened it around each other's shoulders upon the rock were off one at a time."

> **Ann and her father took four of the men aboard their own boat and headed into the open ocean, looking for more survivors.**

Five of the survivors died on the rock, and ten more expired on land after their dramatic rescue. The waves remained merciless the entire time; two babies were swept from their mothers' arms to their deaths, and seven members of a family of thirteen slipped off the rock and drowned. But over an exhausting three-day period from Sunday morning to Tuesday night, more than 180 people were saved in this manner by Ann and George.

Meanwhile, bodies had begun to wash ashore, many of them at Burnt Islands Harbour, just northeast of Wreck Rock. They were gathered and buried by Benjamin Keeping, the first settler of the village. The Harveys' neighbours sent news by boat of the large number of survivors to LaPoile so a rescue ship could come for them.

Captain Sir Richard Grant later reported to Rear Admiral Sir Charles Ogle: " ...a fisherman brought the melancholy intelligence of the wreck of a vessel from Ireland bound to Quebec with immigrants and that many were drowned—a part had reached Port-aux-Basques three leagues distant, but that the majority were near the spot where the vessel struck and would perish for want of subsistence. I instantly made sail..."

By now, Ann, George, and young Tom were dropping with fatigue. In three days they had hardly been out of their small boat; the rescue effort had gone on during the night as well as during daylight hours. Ann rowed the boat against heavy seas, a difficult task.

But her work didn't end there, for now the survivors had to be fed. There is no mention in any of the sparse historical record of Ann's moth-

> Ann Harvey's heroics became widely known once more with the publication of Kevin Major's *Ann and Seamus* (Groundwood, 2003), a fictionalized account of Ann's story told in verse.

er, so we cannot be sure if she was alive at this time. As the oldest female, either Mrs. Harvey or Ann would have been in charge of feeding the survivors. This was a challenging task, given their high numbers and the limited supplies the tiny community had in store. Besides, the nearest merchants were many miles away in Jersey Harbour and Harbour Breton. There were so many people and so little food at Dead Islands that Archdeacon Wix concluded that, had the *Tyne* not showed up, "They might else have only exchanged the perils of the sea for famine upon shore, as the poor shore settlers were very scantily provided."

Indeed, by the time Captain Grant's ship, the HMS *Tyne*, showed up about eight days later, there was no bread, flour or tea left in the Harvey home. It seemed that Ann and her family were facing a winter of subsisting on nothing but saltfish. Captain Grant noticed that there was "not a particle of food" in the little home, and he ordered his crew to amply replenish the Harvey pantry.

Although Ann and her family had saved their lives and tried their best to feed and care for the survivors in the intervening days, the would-be immigrants were in pitiful condition. There were few homes on Dead Islands, so the Harveys and some of the survivors built lean-tos for shelter.

When Captain Grant arrived, he was dismayed at the sight of the survivors. He wrote: "I found 50 men, 30 women and 11 children in the most wretched condition, many of them barely covered with the clothes washed on shore from the wreck, as they had been obliged to strip on the rock to enable the few hands in the boats to drag them through the surf." He noted the deep grief of many of the survivors and the sad fact that some of them still hoped to recover their lost relatives.

Grant's ship took the survivors to St. John's, and news of the heroism of Ann and her father travelled throughout the island and beyond. From Government House, Governor Thomas Cochrane applied to the Royal Humane Society in England for recognition for the family. His request was successful. The Society struck a special medal, which was inscribed to George and presented to Ann by Archdeacon Wix when he visited Dead Islands in 1830. In his journal, Wix described his great pleasure in giving the girl, now nineteen, the award. In addition to the medal, subscribers at Lloyd's, the insurance agents, gave the Harveys the then princely sum of £100. Queen Victoria was said to have written Ann and George a letter in her own handwriting, though it has never been found.

Ann's days as a rescuer of the shipwrecked were not over. On September 4, 1838, the *Rankin* was sailing from Glasgow to Quebec and went aground near the same spot as the *Despatch*. Captain Alexander Mitchell and other survivors of the *Rankin* sent flares into the sky, and these must have been seen by the Harveys. Once again, Ann, who seems to have been still fishing with her father, and George acted the heroes, this time saving six and eight people at a time in their punt. In total, they saved the lives of twenty-five people. This time, however, they seem to have gotten no recompense.

Ann and her family lived in a place where many ships were wrecked, and they almost grew used to burying bodies that washed ashore. There were so many wrecks that a visitor to Isle aux Morts wrote in 1854: "Articles from wrecked ships are to be found in almost every dwelling in the shape of old riggings, spars, masts, sails, ship's bells, rudders, wheels and other items on the outside of the houses, and telescopes, compasses, and portions of incongruous furniture in the interior."

In the early 1840s, Ann married Charles Guillame (Archdeacon Wix's spelling) or Gillam. The town of Gillams on Newfoundland's west coast is probably named for this family. Ann did not live a long life; she died at age forty-nine in 1860.

For a time, Ann was known as the Grace Darling of Newfoundland, after the English girl who, with her father, saved the lives of seamen wrecked on the Northumberland coast. (Ironically, Grace's heroics took place after Ann's.) Then for a long time, Ann's fellow Newfoundlanders seemed to have forgotten her. But on July 17, 1987, the Canadian Coast Guard Ship *Ann Harvey* was christened and commissioned. The next year, a plaque in Ann's memory was unveiled in Isle aux Morts by John Butt, then the province's Minister of Culture, Recreation, and Youth, and Calvin Mitchell, LaPoile MHA.

The medal given to the Harveys by the Royal Humane Society is long lost. But Ann and George's spectacular feat will not be forgotten; if it wasn't for their bravery, more than 200 people might have died.

THE LAST WOMAN HANGED
CATHERINE SNOW

St. John's Courthouse. Photo credit: Garry Cranford.

"She advanced with a firm step and met her fate with remarkable composure," read the *Newfoundlander*. The crowds below were hushed as they watched her body drop. They had come from all over the city to see this, and from Torbay and Petty Harbour, too. There was a sob here and there, an angry cry or two. But most were silent. Many believed it would not come to this. But it had. Now her body, black-clad, in the clothes of the dead, swung in the warm summer breeze. Catherine Mandeville Snow was dead—the last woman to be hanged in Newfoundland.

Snow was born in the late 1700s, probably between 1790 and 1793 in Harbour Grace, Conception Bay. At the time of her birth, the fishery seemed to be in rapid decline, having failed for a number of years. But the Harbour Grace of her youth remained a bustling town, the centre of the bay, the locus of all tradespeople and major shops and industry. She may have learned to read, at least to a rudimentary level, but she probably could not write; this was not an unusual combination in those days.

As a young woman, she moved to Salmon Cove near Port de Grave, also in Conception Bay. There, Catherine took up residence with John William Snow. He was a planter, a fisherman who owned land; a native of Bareneed, he was born around 1793. Well off, he even had servants who used the back stairs. He and Catherine didn't marry at first, but they had children. Eventually they would have seven. After the first three or four, they went to the church and finally tied the knot on October 30, 1828—the day before Hallowe'en.

Despite their little boys and girls and their lack of financial woes, theirs was not a happy union. Researcher Kay Anonsen told the *Newfoundland Herald* in 2001, "They fought all the time, but she fought back. They'd roar away at each other, according to reports, and she would throw things at him, like an iron. Nobody 'reported' him hitting her (though)."

Then, on the night of August 31, 1833, John Snow disappeared. The days passed, and his neighbours on the south side of Port de Grave began to wonder quietly and then out loud if he had committed suicide—or if he had been murdered. Magistrate Robert Pinsent wondered, too, and he launched an investigation. He became very suspicious when he found dried blood on John Snow's fishing stage; he immediately knew there had been foul play.

When asked by the magistrate, Catherine Snow insisted she knew nothing of her husband's whereabouts. But Pinsent was not convinced. He was also suspicious of Tobias Mandeville, Catherine's first cousin, who kept the books for Snow and who was disgruntled with his wages. Besides, Mandeville was said to be having an affair with Catherine. Magistrate Pinsent had another eye on

Arthur Springer[1], one of Snow's indentured servants; according to one account, it was he who was having an affair with Catherine. Both men were considerably younger than the Snows; Mandeville was twenty-four at the time of John Snow's disappearance, while Springer was twenty-seven.

The police brought both men in for questioning and then eavesdropped on them. They heard Springer speak of a conspiracy between the two men and Snow herself. They had shot John Snow, tied him to an anchor, and dumped him in shark-infested waters. When they realized the police knew what had happened, the murderers owned up to it. But Springer maintained Mandeville had shot John Snow, while Mandeville insisted Springer had killed him.

Catherine Snow, meanwhile, had run away to the woods. She hid there, contemplating her options. She must have decided they were few, for she soon decided she had to face the music. She made her way to the new courthouse in Harbour Grace and turned herself in.

Catherine Snow, meanwhile, had run away to the woods. She hid there, contemplating her options.

According to the confessions, John Snow had been shot while going from his boat to his stagehead, but his body was not to be found. On one occasion, Port de Grave harbour was dragged by fifty men in ten boats, but John Snow's watery grave would not give him up.

The trial of Catherine Snow, Tobias Mandeville and Arthur Springer opened in the dead of a St. John's winter on January 10, 1834. Despite the men's confessions, all three pleaded not guilty. Snow and Mandeville were represented by George Henry Emerson, while Springer's lawyer was Bryan Robinson. The attor-

---

1 Who was called Spring in some accounts.

ney-general told the all-male jury, "I can't prove which one fired the shot, but both were present for the murder. As to Catherine Snow, there is no direct or positive evidence of her guilt. But I have a chain of circumstantial evidence to prove her guilt."

The trial was one of the most eventful in Newfoundland history. It lasted twelve hours, during which it was claimed that Snow supplied Springer and Mandeville with her husband's shotgun. The men's testimony, from their confessions, against her was recanted. Then Emerson announced that Snow was pregnant, and she professed that she was entirely innocent of the crime with which she was charged. Not one to put up with any nonsense, Judge Boulton appointed a jury of matrons to confirm the pregnancy. Snow was indeed expecting her eighth child.

The jury returned their verdict in a mere thirty minutes: all three were guilty. There was no question of appeal in those days. The only sentence for their crime was death.

On January 31, 1834, Arthur Springer and Tobias Mandeville were hanged. It was a rare double hanging that drew many spectators from all around the city and beyond. The *Public Ledger* wrote of their deaths in great detail: "Mandeville made his exit from this world but with very little struggling and passed into eternity. His miserable companion endured a strike with human nature of nearly three minutes before animal life became extinct, and after hanging for the space of half an hour, both bodies were taken down and committed to their coffins. It is intended that they be gibbeted again at Spectacle Hill in the neighbourhood of the place where the murder was committed as a salutary warning of the awful consequences of crime."

Many in Newfoundland, especially St. John's, were determined that Snow not meet the same fate. Bishop Michael Fleming, the colourful Catholic leader with a habit of turning every issue into a sectarian one, made Snow a *cause célèbre*. Under his leadership, the Catholic clergy circulated a petition that claimed too many Catholics were being hanged, and that Judge Boulton was particu-larly prejudiced against them. Governor Cochrane ignored the petition, but allowed Snow's hanging to be delayed until her baby was born.

> The attorney-general told the all-male jury: "As to Catherine Snow, there is no direct or positive evidence of her guilt. But I have a chain of circumstantial evidence to prove her guilt."

Meanwhile, Snow languished in jail. She was visited regularly by Father Waldron, who prayed with her, heard her Confession and gave her Holy Communion.

In the early summer of 1834, in the first years of Representative Government, she gave birth to her last child. Then a platform was erected from a second-storey window of a building just east of the present courthouse on Duckworth Street. (The building was later destroyed in one of many fires to strike the city.)

On July 21, crowds gathered on Duckworth Street, waiting with bated breath for the hanging. Some hoped it would not go ahead. Inside Snow's cell, Bishop Fleming celebrated Mass and, more than likely, he and Waldron administered the Last Rites to the doomed woman. She was dressed in her burial clothes, and reportedly screamed and became delirious when she saw herself in the mirror.

Afterwards, she composed herself and walked out on the platform. Her last words were, "I was a wretched woman, but I am as innocent of any participation in the crime of murder as an unborn child." The platform was hauled in, Snow's body dropped into the summer air, and she met her death. According to the *Public Ledger*, "The unhappy woman, after a few brief struggles, passed into another world."

Snow was about forty years old and left eight orphaned children back in Port de Grave. Her body was interred in consecrated ground in the Catholic cemetery at the bottom of Long's Hill, St. John's. The extension of such a gesture to an executed criminal was highly unusual.

It was said that for the next fifty years Snow haunted the courthouse in St. John's. A rock in Port de Grave near where John Snow was shot remained red for many decades.

Snow was the last woman hanged in Newfoundland, and the second-last person subjected to a public hanging—although those convicted of capital crimes were executed in private until the 1940s.

MAKING THIS PLACE OUR OWN

WILLIAM CARSON AND PATRICK MORRIS

In contrast to some of Britain's other overseas possessions, Newfoundland existed in a kind of political neverland in the early part of the 1800s. The island's masters in London still regarded the island as a fishing station, a temporary residence from which the rich cod fishery could be prosecuted. In a way, Newfoundland was akin to a giant floating ship.

And the powers-that-were at Whitehall in London intended to keep it that way. Private property was not allowed. No one was permitted to build a structure within six miles of the shore, except for the purposes of curing, salting, and otherwise processing fish. Fish, a valuable commodity, was all that Newfoundland's British masters cared about, and they guarded their overseas resource jealously.

The island was governed by men sent out from England in the spring for a few months over the summer; they always returned home in the fall. There had never been a resident governor. The law, such as it was, was administered by naval officers who, with their military training, were quick to use force. The island lacked schools, poor relief, marketplaces, roads—in short, all the basic infrastructure of the day that was taken for granted in Britain and even in some of her overseas possessions.

All this might imply that an atmosphere of anarchy and chaos reigned in Newfoundland, and many have made that assumption. But that seems not to have been the case. In 1808, Governor Holloway returned to Newfoundland from England in the spring to find "Harmony and Tranquillity." By this time, there were about 20,000 people living in Newfoundland—year-round, despite legislation that made it difficult to do so—with almost a third of them in St. John's. Officially, however, these people did not exist.

In 1791, John Reeves had demanded a legislature, but his request had been in vain. The idea was also suggested by Governor James Gambier during his 1802–1803 term, but London had not acted upon it.

The status of Newfoundland would change in the 1820s, and again in the 1830s, largely through the actions of two men who chose to make Newfoundland their home: William Carson and Patrick Morris, the former a Protestant Scottish physician, and the latter an Irish Catholic merchant.

Carson was born in Kirkudbrightshire, Scotland in 1770, a mining region, to Margaret MacGlaherty and Samuel Carson, who were an affluent couple. Carson studied medicine at the University of Edinburgh, but, according to Patrick O'Flaherty's research, seems not to have graduated. This, however, did not stop him from practicing in Birmingham and, as O'Flaherty discovered, "acquir(ing) his degree... in the process of crossing the Atlantic." In Birmingham, Carson married local girl Esther Giles, and they had five children; three more were born in Newfoundland, where Esther died young, leaving Carson a widower for more than a quarter century.

William Carson. Photo credit: *Encyclopedia of Newfoundland and Labrador*, Vol. 1.

There were few doctors in Newfoundland in 1808, when Carson immigrated. His first job was as surgeon to soldiers guarding St. John's from the French. He was instrumental in founding the city's first general hospital (there had been one only for soldiers) in 1814: the Newfoundland Hospital. In 1829, he had the dubious honour of performing an autopsy on Shanawdithit, the woman revered in Newfoundland as the last of the Beothuk.

Carson studied the teachings of the English liberal Charles James Fox, who espoused ideas of liberty and human rights, and promoted the notion of a constitution as essential to liberation. In 1812, he published the first of his political pamphlets, in which he criticized the system of non-resident naval governors, decrying their use of force on the civilian population. He accused the governors of poor judgment and bad reasoning, and condemned the legislation that made permanent settlement so difficult.

The authorities did not take these criticisms well; Governor John Duckworth was incensed and considered suing Carson for libel. In the end, the pamphlet cost Carson his job. He even had to fight to get the salary he was owed; in this, he was successful.

In 1813, Carson published another pamphlet called *Reasons for Colonizing the Island of Newfoundland in a Letter Addressed to the Inhabitants*. This time his goal was to politicize Newfoundlanders themselves. He expounded on themes that would become familiar over the years: Newfoundland's ability to become prosperous and the need for adequate constitutional arrangements to make this happen. Again, he roundly condemned the arrogance of Whitehall—the seat of government in London—and the naval governors, especially regarding the prohibitions on settlement.

He wrote: "The only remedy will be found in giving to the people—what is unquestionably their right; a civil government consisting of a Resident Governor, a senate house and a House of Assembly." Governor Richard Keats saw red, calling Carson's text "the poisonous publication and vicious pamphlet."

Meanwhile, Carson's fellow Newfoundlanders had already begun to fight for better services. The year before, a group of St. John's merchants and others had signed a petition requesting new streets, a marketplace, street lighting and other amenities, and sent it to the Prince Regent. They got no reply, but the action showed that the settlers had decided to stay—they had decided Newfoundland was their home, whether London realized it or not.

Carson continued his campaign with a series of letters to the editor of the *Newfoundland* newspaper. He worked with the Merchants' Society to put test cases through the courts, challenging and defeating the laws against erecting permanent buildings. The result of these court cases was that, for the first time, Newfoundlanders got land grants to build houses.

> Governor Richard Keats saw red, calling Carson's text "the poisonous publication and vicious pamphlet."

Carson was not alone now in putting pressure on the absentee governors, and the last one, Keats, left in 1816. This was a huge step toward permanence on the island, although representative and responsible government were still some way away. The first governor who over-wintered was Admiral Pickmore, who died in the process.

In 1824, Newfoundland finally became a British colony, but she was still ruled solely by the governor. Carson wanted representative government; up until the 1830s, he opposed responsible government, or full self-government for Newfoundland. His ambitions for the island were apparently limited; unlike some who would come after him, he was not a Newfoundland nationalist, driven by emotion. In a speech, he said modestly, "I ask only for roads, bridges, and schools to make Newfoundland happy, glorious and free."

Patrick Morris. Photo credit: *Encyclopedia of Newfoundland and Labrador*, Vol. 3.

His colleague, Patrick Morris, would go further. Unlike Carson's dogmatism, Morris's political actions were a direct response to conditions and events in Newfoundland, particularly as they related to the legal system and the many injustices that occurred.

> His colleague, Patrick Morris, would go further. Unlike Carson's dogmatism, Morris's political actions were a direct response to conditions and events in Newfoundland...

Morris was born in County Waterford, Ireland in 1789 and came to Newfoundland in the early 1800s to work as a clerk for Luke Maddock, a merchant from his home county. By 1810, he was in business for himself, shipping cod and oil back to Ireland and making a good living at it. Later, his export business expanded and he shipped many types of goods—building supplies, coal, household goods, food—to England, Germany, Poland, and what are now the Maritime provinces. By the 1820s, he owned five schooners and a large passenger trade.

Although he was a wealthy man, the event that galvanized Morris involved two of Newfoundland's poorest livyers. James Lundrigan and Philip Butler were two Catholic fishermen unable to pay their debts. Lundrigan owed £13 to a local merchant. For this, he was evicted from his house with his wife and four children. Then he was stripped of his shirt, tied to a flake, and flogged with a cat-o'-nine-tails until he collapsed into an epileptic seizure. Butler was given twelve lashes, and the doors of his house were broken down, his wife and three children forcibly evicted.

> **Then he was stripped of his shirt, tied to a flake, and flogged with a cat-o'-nine-tails until he collapsed into an epileptic seizure.**

By this point, Morris was the first Catholic President of the Benevolent Irish Society (the organization had been formed by the Crown in 1806)—he remained in the position for fifteen years. In reaction to the Lundrigan-Butler incident, he headed up a committee that called for reform. As Carson had done, he began to publish pamphlets. His first was *Observations on the Government, Trade, Fisheries, and Agriculture in Newfoundland*.

Meanwhile, Carson's general attitude toward the many poor people living on the island was at best ambiguous. Some sources, including Joseph Smallwood's glowing essays on the doctor, claimed he was generous to those in need, though not a rich man himself. On the other hand, O'Flaherty says Carson's name did not appear on the list of subscribers donating to the poor following the economy's collapse after the Napoleonic Wars. Further, Carson once made a speech in which he indicated that poverty itself served as a good motivator.

In March 1824, determined that there would never be a repeat of the Lundrigan-Butler incident, Morris and fellow reformer William Dawe travelled to London to press for judicial reform.

Three months later, the Judicature Act was passed. The Act provided for the appointment of qualified judges and a civil governor, and reforms to the Supreme Court. In addition, there were improvements to property and settlement rights. That same year, Newfoundland finally became a British colony, but she was still ruled solely by the governor.

Morris, Dawe and other reformers immediately started agitating for a legislature.

It was a time of change in England; the mother country got a new King in 1820, George IV, and it was a good time to press for reforms. Morris saw this. In 1825, Newfoundland was granted an Executive Council, appointed by the Governor. The Executive Council could advise the Crown and frame legislation. It was a small step forward, but what was significant was how quickly the steps were being made.

Morris was not satisfied with the progress thus far. In 1828, he published the pamphlet *Arguments to Prove the Policy and Necessity for Granting to Newfoundland a Constitutional Government.* Finally, in 1832, the efforts of the Newfoundland reformers paid off when Newfoundland got a constitution and representative government was instituted under Governor Thomas Cochrane. There were nine electoral districts with fifteen members, and an appointed six-member Board of Council (or Legislative Council), which could accept or reject any bills. Final authority rested with the British House of Commons. Men (but not, of course, women) over age twenty-one who had lived in Newfoundland more than one year could vote; to stand for election, the residency requirement was two years.

In the November 5, 1832 election, Carson ran for one of the three St. John's seats, but lost. Later, however, he was acclaimed in a by-election. He was re-elected and became Speaker of the House of Assembly in 1837, then a much more powerful position than it is now. He continued to press for reforms for Newfoundland, and explained his approach in the *Patriot*: "Agitation must be kept up— the high spirits of a high-minded people must be cherished and supported—they must be aroused to the pure love of liberty, to the utter detestation of all tyrants and of all manacles—Submission never gained a point in politics—it has only the effect to confirm pride and foster presumption."

Morris's approach was radically different from that of Carson, who promoted evolutionary change and urged people to submit, lest violence result. A typical Irishman, Morris had great faith in the power of words to convince. On August 25, 1837, he made a famous speech in the House, "On Moving for a Committee to Enquire into the Administration of Justice." So impressed with it were his fellow members, the government printed and distributed it, costing them £22. Occasionally, Morris borrowed from Shakespeare—*Hamlet* or *King Lear*; in protest of the ban on building, he once referred to "the pelting of the pitiless storm." Like his countryman Jonathan Swift (parliamentarian and author *of Gulliver's Travels*), he resorted to satire at times.

In 1838, Carson, Morris and other Newfoundland officials travelled to Britain to lobby for better co-operation between the House of Assembly and the Legislative Council. They also wanted the despised Henry Boulton, hostile as he was to the island's House of Assembly, removed from his position as Chief Justice of the Supreme Court. Morris, who never minced words (he once called the British government "ignorant" and "disinterested"), told the London authorities that Boulton "trampled on the rights and privileges and immunities of the British subject." He was ejected from the court.

By now, Morris was a Member of the House of Assembly as well, having been elected in 1836. the *Patriot* called him "the most popular man in Newfoundland." He was an MHA until 1840, when he became Colonial Treasurer, a position he held until his death nine years later.

Morris once said of Carson, "It was he who first taught them to know their rights—it was he who first moved to their rulers that they had the spirit to assert and maintain them." But Carson's legacy is also one of disillusionment with politics and politicians. It was largely as a result of his actions that Britain suspended the Newfoundland constitution in 1840. Carson had gotten into a fracas with physician Edward Kielley; the conflict led to charges of assault, false imprisonment, threats, and lawsuits. The reformers (i.e. Carson) were seen to place eminent citizens with whom they disagreed in custody.

It would be wrong, however, to lay the entire blame of the dissolution of Newfoundland's constitution at Carson's feet. It also came about because of a contentious by-election in late 1840. The campaign and voting was marked by extreme violence. In addition, there was no return for Carbonear, and the election result was declared void. Governor Prescott did not call another by-election, since there was a general election scheduled for 1841. Whitehall was critical of him because he had delayed sending in the troops; their preference would have been to send them in at the first whiff of trouble. Subsequently, the British government ordered Prescott to dissolve the legislature and suspend the constitution; he did so on April 26, 1841.

Established governments may get away with this kind of undemocratic behaviour—jailing their enemies, campaign violence, and missing polls—but new ones in the colonies never do; they are always held to a higher standard. So the eight-year-old Newfoundland constitution was suspended.

In 1842, the Legislative Council and the House of Assembly were amalgamated. Now there were fifteen elected and ten appointed members, with a separate Executive Council. Carson was re-elected, but by now, Governor Sir John Harvey had appointed him to the Executive Council. Carson had become a convert to the responsible government cause, believing, finally, that Newfoundlanders were capable of ruling themselves.

From his deathbed the next year, Carson issued the call for all Newfoundlanders to fight for responsible government. With the exception of a few—as we shall see—they didn't. Perhaps they were disillusioned with Carson himself, and/or with the merchants he had allied himself with as he promoted the cause. Historian Judge D.W. Prowse described him as "dogmatic" and "self-opinionated"—he does not seem to have had the attractive personal characteristics of his colleague, Patrick Morris. His "restless, driving ambition," to use O'Flaherty's words, may have been off-putting for many Newfoundlanders, too. The island was a place that required co-operation and a sense of community; Carson was a man who had applied for a letters patent that would have given him exclusive rights to hunt whales in coastal waters. This may have struck in the craw as simple greed. The dirtiness of the Kielley affair surely left a bad taste in the mouth, too, especially given its far-reaching result.

Nevertheless, Carson's hometown in Scotland honoured him in a special ceremony on one of his visits there. In the British Museum in London, he is recog-

THE WILLIAM CARSON

Built in 1954, the *William Carson* was a passenger, vehicle, and cargo ferry, more than 8,000 tons. The *Carson* sank off Labrador on June 3, 1977, when ice tore through the hull on the starboard side. All 128 people on board were saved.

nized as "the Parent of Agriculture in Newfoundland"; by 1831, he had a 116-acre farm, and never tired of expounding on the vast potential of agriculture on the island. In 1847, he wrote a pamphlet called *A Short Review of the History, Government, Constitution, Fishery, and Agriculture of Newfoundland.* At age seventy-one, he became president of Newfoundland's first Agricultural Society.

Morris, too, promoted agriculture on the island. He operated the ninety-two-acre Cottage Farm on the north side of Quidi Vidi Lake in St. John's. He fought to have restrictions on agriculture removed, but some of the prohibitions on land ownership remained throughout his political tenure. Yet by 1840, there were some 300 farms on the Northeast Avalon alone.

The Newfoundland public seemed to have had much more affection for Morris. His funeral was said to be the largest Newfoundland had ever seen. The *Patriot* wrote, "...in the whole course of his life, Mr. Morris lived less for himself than for the welfare of his adopted country." The St. John's *Times*, which opposed him politically, would not concede that Newfoundland was any better off for his actions, but did remark on his "sincerity and goodness." The *Ledger* remembered "(the) warm interest he took in the welfare of the community."

Morris left Newfoundlanders a legacy of thought and rhetoric that is still very much with us. He rightly identified such serious problems as the loss of capital to Poole merchants and others as a problem that stunted

> But [Morris] almost entirely blamed the woes of Newfoundlanders on others—outsiders—thus engendering a collective helplessness that is so often the lingering after-effect of colonialism.

development on the island. But he almost entirely blamed the woes of Newfoundlanders on others—outsiders—thus engendering a collective helplessness that is so often the lingering after-effect of colonialism. He also emphasized the notion that it was always outsiders who reaped the benefits of Newfoundland's resources; without them, the island would enjoy almost unimagined prosperity.

PHILIP LITTLE AND ROBERT PARSONS

Robert John Parsons. Photo credit: *The Book of Newfoundland*, Vol. 5.

Among those agitating for Responsible Government throughout the 1840s, two of the most prominent were Philip Francis Little and Robert John Parsons.

A descendant of bush-borns, Robert John Parsons was a Harbour Grace native, born in 1802 or 1803. He married Eliza Flood in 1835 and, as a young man, apprenticed with the *Royal Gazette* before moving to the *Public Ledger*. He founded the *Newfoundland Patriot* in 1833; the paper later became the *Patriot*, and then the *Terra Nova Herald*. Parsons believed in the power of words, particularly the written word, to convince minds and bring about change. Throughout his life, he would use it to great effect.

As a commentary on the Newfoundland legal system and its benchers, Parsons once wrote a satirical article on the virtues of hanging. It read in part: "We understand that a lecture was delivered in the courthouse yesterday to the Grand Petit Juries on the opening of the Central Circuit Court by the President of the Council in the capacity of the Chief Judge, on the very great benefits which hanging of people confers on society—arising no doubt, from its sedative effects upon the human system, which to the uninitiated are truly astonishing..."

For refusing to name the author of this piece, Parsons was charged and given the choice of three months in jail or a fine of £50. Parsons chose the jailhouse, and, while he waited there, townspeople fumed. They were so angry, the authorities had to put a military garrison on alert. The people collected 5,000 signatures and fired off a protest to the Colonial Office in London. Within a few days, Parsons emerged a free man. Upon his release, a grand dinner was held in his honour.

In an 1843 by-election, Parsons was elected to the Amalgamated Assembly for St. John's. A Liberal, he made his mark by attacking the establishment. Like Patrick Morris, he constantly criticized the power wielded over Newfoundland from outside, and as a Member of the Assembly he tirelessly promoted Responsible Government for Newfoundland. Over and over, his newspaper, the *Patriot*, editorialized on the need for self-rule for the island.

In 1851, Parsons presented a resolution to the Amalgamated Assembly calling for Responsible Government. It passed easily and was forwarded to London. The British reply was the same one that colonies would get for decades: Newfoundland was "not ready." Several similar resolutions were rejected. Governor LeMarchant grew hostile to the elected members, and even recommended to Lord Grey, the Colonial Secretary, that the Assembly be abolished and Newfoundland returned to direct rule.

John Kent and Ambrose Shea were among those who agitated for Responsible Government. Besides Parsons, they would soon be joined by Philip Little. Like William Carson and Patrick Morris, Little was not born in Newfoundland. He was born in Charlottetown, Prince Edward Island in 1824; his parents, Cornelius Little and Brigid Costin, were Irish emigrants who had become prosperous in the New World. Little studied law under Charles Young, and then surprised everyone by immigrating to Newfoundland, where he had maternal relatives. He was the first Roman Catholic lawyer in St. John's and, not surprisingly, became involved with the Benevolent Irish Society.

Little turned his attention to politics, getting the support of the Roman Catholic bishop, Michael Anthony Fleming, who was never one to shy away from politics, and then his successor, Bishop Mullock. At only twenty-six, and after spending only half a dozen years in Newfoundland, Little was elected as a Liberal in an 1850 by-election in St. John's.

Philip Little. Photo credit:
Encyclopedia of Newfoundland and Labrador, Vol. 3.

Like Parsons, Little did not take British rejection of the Responsible Government resolutions lying down. The House wanted to deliver a message calling for a form of self-rule to London, but it didn't trust Governor Ker Baillie Hamilton to deliver it, as protocol would have dictated. The members decided to send Little and Parsons to Britain to meet with the Duke of Newcastle, the Colonial Secretary, to make representation. The Executive Council, however, wouldn't authorize the use of public funds for this purpose. Little and Parsons would not be stopped, however; they made the trip on private monies.

In London, they made a valuable ally, John Hume, a British Member of Parliament, who agreed to present a resolution in their support to the House of Commons. Little and Parsons quieted the Duke of Newcastle's fears: yes, they told him, there are, in fact, qualified men to govern in Newfoundland; no, they said, the legislature will not be dominated by the Roman Catholics and their church. Both men left the meeting feeling confident.

Back in Newfoundland, it took some months to sort out the contentious issues of electoral districts, including numbers of seats and religious balance, as well as pensions for those government officials who would lose their jobs. In 1855, Responsible Government came to Newfoundland. It was a vast improvement on the Amalgamated Assembly, but it was far from perfect. Absolute authority still rested with Britain, whose wishes would still be communicated through the governor. The Executive Council, however, would be responsible to the elected House of Assembly.

At only thirty-one, Philip Little became Newfoundland's first prime minister. His government held eighteen of the thirty seats;

LITTLE'S AND PARSONS'S FAMILY CONNECTIONS

Robert Parsons's son, Robert, became a Liberal Member of the House of Assembly, like his father before him.

Philip Little's younger brother, Joseph Little, also immigrated to Newfoundland from Prince Edward Island. He, too, entered Newfoundland politics, and became Chief Justice in 1898.

On the one hundredth anniversary of the granting of Responsible Government, Philip Little's youngest son, P.J. Little, visited Newfoundland at the invitation of the Government of Newfoundland.

---

the governor was Sir Charles Darling, Ambrose Shea was Speaker (then a powerful position), and John Kent was Colonial Secretary. Little was in office only from 1855 to 1858 but his government was a busy one. He created a Board of Revenue, a Board of Works, and made provisions for the establishment of a Newfoundland Savings Bank. Little signed a Reciprocity Treaty with the United States, and incorporated the New York, Newfoundland, and London Telegraph Company. Legislation passed included the Naturalization of Aliens Act, the Roads Act, an Act for the Protection of the Herring Fishery, and several education-related Acts.

The undisputed highlight of Little's tenure, however, was the Labouchere Despatch, sometimes referred to as Newfoundland's Magna Carta.

In 1857, the British and French governments, without Newfoundland's input or consultation, signed a convention which extended French fishing rights in Newfoundland. Under the Anglo-French Convention, the French could now fish from Cape St. John on the northeast coast to Cape Norman. It also gave French fishing ships access to five harbours scattered throughout Newfoundland: Port aux Choix; Small Harbour; Port au Port; Red Island; and Codroy Island.

The undisputed highlight of Little's tenure, however, was the Labouchere Despatch, sometimes referred to as Newfoundland's Magna Carta.

The Little government responded quickly, with an unequivocally worded statement partly written by Parsons. It read: "We deem it our duty, most respectfully, to protest in the most solemn manner against any attempt to alienate any portion of our fisheries or our soil to any foreign power, without the consent of the local legislature. As our fishery and territorial rights constitute the basis of our commerce and of our social and political existence, as they are our birthright and the legal inheritance of our children, we cannot, under any circumstances, assent to the terms of the convention; we therefore earnestly entreat that the Imperial Government will take no steps to bring this treaty into operation, but will permit the trifling privileges that remain to us to continue impaired."

Prime Minister Little, Robert Parsons, Opposition Leader Hugh Hoyles, and MHAs Lawrence O'Brien and James Tobin travelled to Britain to deliver their strong message. They must have made a favourable impression, because the LaBouchere Despatch was the result. It read: "The proposals contained in the Convention having been unequivocally refused by the Colony; they will of course fall to the ground. And you are authorized to give such assurance as you may think proper that the consent of the community of Newfoundland is regarded by Her Majesty's Government as the essential preliminary to any modification of their territorial or maritime rights."

This message was sent from Henry La-Bouchere, the British Colonial Secretary, to

THE PRIME MINISTERS OF NEWFOUNDLAND

Philip Little, 1855–1858
John Kent, 1858–1861
Hugh Hoyles, 1861–1865
Frederick Carter, 1865–1870
Charles Fox Bennett, 1870–1874
Frederick Carter, 1874–1878
William Whiteway, 1878–1885
Robert Thorburn, 1885–1889
William Whiteway, 1889–1894
Augustus Goodridge, April–Dec. 1894
Daniel Greene, Dec. 1894–Feb. 1895
James Winter, 1897–1900
Robert Bond, 1900–1909
Edward Morris, 1909–1917
William Lloyd, Jan. 1918–May 1919
Michael P. Cashin, May–Nov. 1919
Richard Anderson Squires, 1919–1923
William Warren, July 1923–May 1924
Albert Hickman, May–June 1924
Walter Monroe, 1924–1928
Frederick Alderdice, August–Nov. 1928
Richard Anderson Squires, 1928–1932
Frederick Alderdice, 1932–1934

the Governor of Newfoundland. It signified a change in the balance of power: for the first time, Britain would actually ascertain the opinions and viewpoints of the Newfoundland government before making any decisions that would lead to policy changes. The words "essential preliminary" are important and mark a real change from the disrespect that London showed toward Newfoundland when the Colonial Office dissolved the island's constitution a few short years before.

...for the first time, Britain would actually ascertain the opinions and viewpoints of the Newfoundland government before making any decisions that would lead to policy changes.

The next year, Little resigned, citing "poor health," but a year later, he became Chief Justice. As a politician, he had often said, "Handle the worm as if you mean him no harm." Accordingly, one *Evening Telegram* writer theorized that "his early retirement from politics may have been partly caused by his desire not to have the milk of human kindness turn sour in him."

In 1864, he married Mary Jane Holdright, from a wealthy Irish family, and the new family moved to Ireland. There, Little became the father of eight sons and three daughters, and, to no one's surprise, fought for Home Rule for Ireland. Little died in late October, 1897.

Parsons had a much longer tenure in Newfoundland politics, almost four decades. Some of his colleagues attended the 1864 Quebec Conference to discuss the merits of uniting the British North American colonies. Ambrose Shea went, and returned a convert. But Parsons remained bitterly opposed to Confederation, fearing, rather prophetically, that if she joined the Canadas, Newfoundland would become "an outharbour of another province." In Newfoundland, the anti-confederate movement was led by Charles Bennett Fox and won the 1869 election.

Parsons's fervour for Newfoundland never wavered. He was one of the founders of the Natives Society, which promoted just treatment for native-born Newfoundlanders in their own land. The Society also served as a watchdog, criticizing what it said was the corruption and abuses of power of British officials in Newfoundland. Parsons viewed Newfoundland as very welcoming to outsiders, too much so in that

> "Newfoundland isolated?" [Parsons] once bellowed. "How is that? Our argosies whiten every sea!"

native-born Newfoundlanders seemed disadvantaged in acquiring positions of authority both inside and outside the government. He resisted the confederates' argument that the island was isolated. "Newfoundland isolated?" he once bellowed. "How is that? Our argosies whiten every sea!"

Parsons was one of the first to refer to Newfoundlanders as a people, as a nation. In the pages of the *Patriot*, and in the House of Assembly, he tried to make the natives and others see that Newfoundland was a nation like England or France, and that it deserved the same respect.

A Protestant, Parsons was always even-handed in his treatment of Catholic news and events—so much so that some writers have erroneously dubbed the *Patriot* the Catholic paper. Like Morris and Little, he was against the sectarianism that other elites on the island tried hard to ferment. He died on June 20, 1883.

CAPTAIN WILLIAM JACKMAN

Photo credit: *Encyclopedia of Newfoundland and Labrador*, Vol. 3.

The October Gale of 1867 was one of legendary proportions. It roared across the coast of Labrador, wrecking forty-two ships, and taking forty lives. Though this loss of life was devastating enough, it would have taken thirty more had it not been for four brave men: Labradorians John Holwell; his brother Samuel; Robert Mesher; and the undisputed leader of the rescue effort, Captain William Jackman.

Jackman was born on May 20, 1837, in Renews. He was the first child of Catherine Johnson, and Thomas Jackman, who was a schooner owner and skipper descended from a long line of Southern Shore natives. At age fifteen, William joined his father on the colourfully named *Fanny Bloomer*. In less than three years, he qualified as a master mariner. From age seventeen to his mid-twenties, he was a captain on Bowring Brothers' schooners *Shipworth, Sarah Ann* and *Margaret.* His father had worked for the same company.

The young man's future seemed bright indeed. At twenty-one, Jackman married Bridget Burbridge of Trepassey. They had four sons and two daughters.

In the fall of 1867, Jackman found himself on Spotted Island, on the southern Labrador coast. The island was named after the spotted seal that frequented the cold Labrador water. The Meshers, Holwells, Dysons, and other families lived on the southeast corner of the island in summer so they could access the rich fishing grounds. In winter, they repaired to Porcupine Bay to be near the woods and fur-bearing animals. They were the descendants of British men and Inuit women. They were Métis.

Every summer, livyers from Newfoundland's northeast coast came to Griffin Harbour on the north side of Spotted Island, to fish. They often brought their whole families, and even chickens for eggs and goats to milk. The Newfoundlanders returned home each fall, usually with a full load of fish. The two groups, the Métis and the Newfoundlanders, tended to keep their distance from each other.

In October, 1867, the *Sea Clipper,* a seventy-two-foot schooner, was on its way back to Conception Bay. She had a heavy load of salt cod and a human cargo of souls worn out from a summer of non-stop work. When the storm came up, Captain Albert Rideout tried to make port at Spotted Island, but the winds and waves were so high that his ship collided with the *Loon,* another Conception Bay schooner. The *Loon* was slightly smaller than the *Sea Clipper,* and carried fifteen men and women on their way to Spotted Island and the ships that would take them home to their villages in Conception Bay.

Even after the boats broke free from each other, they remained in danger. The *Sea Clipper* then hit sharp rocks 600 feet from the shores of Spotted Island.

The most detailed account of what happened next comes from Eldon Drodge's book *Jackman* (Jesperson, 2000), which contains photographs and genealogical data. Jackman saw what was happening from his place onshore, and, with all his seagoing experience, he judged that it was far too rough to launch a punt. It would only be a matter of time before the *Sea Clipper* was swallowed by the sea and her passengers with her. Jackman saw that there was only one way to save them.

One of few Newfoundland fishermen who could swim, Jackman stripped off most of his clothes and threw himself into the cold Labrador sea. He swam out to the *Sea Clipper* and plucked one of the passengers from the floundering boat, carrying him to Spotted Island on his back.

According to Drodge, Jackman rescued six people in this manner, in half an hour. By now, John and Samuel Holwell and Robert Mesher had rigged a rope to a large rock on the shore. Then they plunged into the water and went part of the way out. As Jackman swam to the *Sea Clipper* and fetched a passenger, the Spotted Island men took the rescued person and brought him back through the water to the beach.

When Jackman thought he'd gotten the last person, someone mentioned "poor Myra," a woman who lay in a cabin in the schooner; she had been injured in the collision with the *Loon*, and they had given her up for dead. Although he was utterly spent,

Jackman dove into the sea again and went back for her. As the *Newfoundlander* reported this a month later, "'Living or dead,' said Captain Jackman, when he heard of her, 'I'll not leave her there,'" and once again he flung himself amid the waves and again reached the shore, supporting the frame of this poor exhausted woman.

The whole rescue effort lasted two and a half hours. The *Sea Clipper*, meanwhile, lasted another hour, longer than Jackman thought she would. Myra Batten, the injured woman, did not live, however. She expired two days later on Spotted Island. According to the *Veteran Magazine*, "She lived long enough to invoke the blessing of heaven on her brave rescuer."

Jackman was nonchalant about his great feat and soon went back to work. From 1867 to 1876, he was in charge of the *Hawk* and the *Eagle*, the Bowring Brothers' sealing steamers. It was here, at sea fishing and sealing, that he felt most at home.

He was reluctant to accept the accolades that came his way when his heroics were made known. He asked his brother to attend on his behalf a ceremony in his honour, and only later, and perhaps with reservations, ended up going himself. He seems to have come by all this honestly. According to Drodge, his father's only public comment on his son's bravery was, "You know, if William didn't go back for that woman, I think I'd disown him." In 1868, Jackman told *The Youth's Companion* he only did his duty. It was likely the same for the Holwells and Robert Mesher.

All four men were awarded medals by the Royal Humane Society; the Spotted Island men were given bronze medals, and Jackman got a silver medal. The Society also gave Jackman a diploma. In Newfoundland, he was celebrated in a commissioned poem by Marcus Hopkins. The last two stanzas read:

Yet none too soon for not long thence with a resounding roar,
The Sea Clipper *was rent in twain, and then was seen no more;*
And on their knees in grateful prayer they gave thanks for him so brave,
Who spared not himself to save them all from a certain watery grave.

Many are the sagas about men who go down to the sea,
Of superhuman strength and fears and deeds of bravery;
But the name of William Jackman forever more will stand,
Among the immortal heroes in the annals of Newfoundland.

Amazingly, the *Sea Clipper* rescue was not Jackman's only memorable feat. In 1869, just two years after the rescue, he made no less than a record three trips to the ice in the sealing ship *Hawk*. He performed the same feat in 1873, in the *Eagle*. In addition, Jackman was one of the founding members of the Star of the Sea.

THE STAR OF THE SEA

The Star of the Sea was founded on February 28, 1871, in St. John's as a social organization for Newfoundland's Roman Catholic fishermen, under the patronage of the Virgin Mary (*Stella Maris*). Father Daniel Lynch was its first spiritual director, and its three lay leaders were all sealing captains: William Jackman; William Ryan; and Captain Cummins. More than 1,500 men joined in the first six months and, within a few years, there were branches throughout the island. Society activities included sports, charitable assistance, and entertainment, such as theatrical productions. While non-Catholics were accepted as associate members for many years, the rules were amended to allow them to become full members in 1989. According to the *Encyclopedia of Newfoundland and Labrador*, there were 500 members in the St. John's club in the early 1990s, the largest number in some years.

Jackman did not live a long life, some say because of the bat-
tering his body took in the wild Labrador Sea. He died on February
25, 1877, at thirty-nine, after a gradual weakening that seems to
have had some of the symptoms of cancer.

Although the role of the Spotted Island men in the rescue is
usually overlooked, Jackman himself has not been forgotten. On
September 8, 1992, Canada Post issued a stamp in his honour,
showing him leading a rope, about to enter the sea. It is inaccurate,
in that it pictures him with his shirt on; witnesses said he removed
almost all his clothes. He is depicted as a strong, bulky man; on the
stamp, he turns back to face the viewer. This stamp was issued as
part of a series honouring Canadian heroes.

In 1999, the Captain William Jackman Museum and
Interpretation Centre was opened in the skipper's hometown of
Renews, in a former school. In this way, a new generation was intro-
duced to a remarkable Newfoundlander.

A MAN OF HIS TIME

SIR WILFRED
THOMASON GRENFELL

Photo credit: Grenfell
Historical Society.

"The best beloved missionary in the world" was how the U.S. publication *The North American Review* described Sir Wilfred Grenfell in 1928. The compliment says much, both about the man and the age in which he lived. Grenfell's life was one that mixed philanthropy and missionary zeal with the physical daring and taste for adventure akin to that of the great explorers.

His work, in regions that were considered some of the poorest and most underprivileged of the Western hemisphere, was performed as the times dictated—on an international stage. And before his death, he was heaped with many honours, including a knighthood.

Wilfred Thomason Grenfell was born in the English fishing village of Parkgate, near Chester on England's northwest coast, on

February 28, 1865. The fourth son of a Church of England minister and teacher, Grenfell was an athletic and free-spirited youth who spent much of his formative years on the water.

In 1882, the family moved to London, and the following year, Wilfred began to study medicine in a London hospital. Tending wards in London's East End and treating sailors who had been in brawls or fallen on hard times, two themes of his life began to emerge: the welfare of seamen; and a dislike of drink.

One other formative influence would complete the picture of the man Grenfell would become. Returning one evening from a maternity case in East London in 1883, the young student doctor noticed a large tent in a field near the street. He went to investigate, and found he had stumbled across an evangelist meeting being conducted by the famous American preacher D.L. Moody. As he stayed and listened, the young Grenfell felt himself called. As he later remembered,

...the young student doctor noticed a large tent in a field near the street. He went to investigate, and found he had stumbled across an evangelist meeting...

"What I now believe that D.L. Moody did for me was just to show that under all the sham and externals of religion was a vital call in the world for things that I could do."

Not surprisingly in light of this new zeal, when Grenfell graduated in 1888, he joined the National Mission to Deep Sea Fishermen. In serving the fishermen of the North Sea, Grenfell began to develop a medical philosophy, in which both poverty and alcohol were inextricably linked to physical ill health. "The visits to fishermen's homes in our seaports showed that poverty was the chief factor in actual physical abnormalities," he told an audience of physicians in Philadelphia in 1930. "One cannot prevent poverty with vaccines, or destroy it with antiseptics." He was particularly disgusted by the fact that good wages would also be thrown away on spirits and beer, further hampering a healthy lifestyle.

It was with the Mission in 1892 that Grenfell was sent to investigate conditions in the Labrador fishery, which involved hundreds of Newfoundlanders from Conception, Trinity and Bonavista Bays who fished in Labrador each summer.

He found what he described as "a large scattered English-speaking population who fished only from the land; in which no resident doctor, trained nurse or dispensary had ever been known." So struck was Grenfell by the want he had seen, he persuaded the Mission to let him return the following year with two doctors and two nurses. With the help of St. John's authorities, he set up a first hospital on the Labrador coast at Battle Harbour, which lies at the eastern entrance of the Strait of Belle Isle. A second medical base was soon added at Indian Harbour, 200 miles farther north.

But Grenfell believed that the health of families in the fishery was ultimately dependent on their social and economic condition. Soon, he became active in grassroots politics, helping to organize a fishermen's co-operative at Red Bay, Labrador in 1895. Grenfell had become a fierce opponent of the truck system, by which fishermen would be outfitted and given supplies on credit for the season by the merchant, who in turn then effectively "owned" the catch. Grenfell believed the perpetual debt to the merchant was a key factor that kept fishermen in poverty and want.

> Grenfell had become a fierce opponent of the truck system, by which fishermen would be outfitted and given supplies on credit...

Grenfell returned to England between 1897 and 1899, but when he came back, it was with renewed vigour. Within ten years, there were eight fishermen's co-operatives established along the coast and the first St. Anthony–based hospital was opened in 1905.

Grenfell fell out with the National Mission to Help North Sea Fishermen back in England over a number of issues, particularly those which smacked of political action, such as his organization of co-operatives and his promotion of local crafts. The Mission was also uncomfortable with Grenfell's own dynamic form of fundraising, which involved touring North America in the summer. It was with the Mission's blessing, however, that Grenfell's activities became a separate operation in 1912, under the banner The International Grenfell Association (IGA). Along with continued successful fundraising, the IGA expanded and, by 1914, administered four hospitals and six nursing stations along the Labrador and Northern Newfoundland coasts. Over 6,000 patients a year received treatment.

Grenfell himself met the growing success and demand of his own mission with an ever-increasing zeal, and was helped in all his fundraising and administrative duties by his wife Anne Elizabeth Caldwell MacClanahan of Chicago, whom he married in 1909.

Grenfell's image as a man of action added a touch of glamour to his quickly growing international reputation. There were many magazines and periodicals hungry for tales of intrepid and noble adventure, and Grenfell was tailor-made for such copy. It was said that in one winter he covered 1,500 miles behind his sled dogs in his ceaseless care for the sick.

On Easter Sunday in April 1908 came an incident that sealed his reputation as an icon of adventure, as well as medicine. Receiving news that a boy on whom he had operated was sick with blood poisoning sixty miles from St. Anthony on Brent Island, Grenfell ignored advice and rode out on his sled to give medical treatment.

This was the season when ice was breaking up. A shortcut over the bay proved almost fatal, as he became stranded upon an ice pan that began drifting out to sea. In imminent danger of freezing, Grenfell stabbed his three dogs to death, wrapped their hides around his shoulders for warmth, and made a windbreak out of the carcasses. He managed to survive a night without freezing. Then, amazingly for such a sparsely populated area, Grenfell was spotted through a telescope and rescued.

This tale of amazing deeds and a near-impossible escape, powered perhaps by divine intervention, contributed greatly to the Grenfell mystique, particularly when he published a best-selling account, *Adrift on an Ice Pan*, in 1909. As if all this were not colourful enough, the story also boasts a particularly poignant note of sacrifice. Soon after the adventure, Grenfell affixed a tablet to his house: "To the memory of those three noble dogs, Moody [named presumably after the evangelist who had so affected Grenfell in the East End of London], Watch and Spy, whose lives were given for mine on the ice, April 21st, 1908."

In the teens and the 1920s, Grenfell's reputation continued to grow. He was regularly welcomed by benevolent societies and med-

Lady Grenfell married Wilfred before she had seen either St. Anthony or Labrador. Although she threw herself into her husband's work, she never enjoyed living in St. Anthony. As a woman of some standing and wealth in Chicago, she was instrumental in gaining many new patrons. She founded an educational fund for Newfoundland and Labrador students to the U.S. and Canada, and was active in arranging benefit concerts in the U.S. to raise funds for the IGA. In later years, when her husband's health was declining, she took over more of the administrative duties, presiding over the Dogteam Tavern in Vermont, where Grenfell's Mission found an outlet for the crafts manufactured in Labrador. In Sir Wilfred's last trip to St. Anthony in 1939, he buried Lady Grenfell's ashes on Fox Farm Hill. His own ashes were brought to join her after his death.

ical universities to speak and, in 1928, received the ultimate accolade in his own country with a knighthood. The year before, a fully-equipped modern hospital had been build in St. Anthony.

In the early 1930s, he suffered a series of heart attacks and, in 1935, he and Lady Grenfell retired to Vermont. Lady Grenfell died in 1938, and, after one final return to St. Anthony the following year in which he was received as a hero, Grenfell himself died on October 9, 1940. In 1970, a statue of

> Always looking for ways to bring healthy sources of nutrition and clothing to the people of the Northern Peninsula and Labrador, Grenfell tried to introduce reindeer to the area, landing in St. Anthony with his first herd in 1908. The herd grew steadily for a time, and the experiment seemed to be working, but eventually numbers fell off, possibly due to poaching, and the remainder of the shrinking herd was taken to Quebec in 1920.

Grenfell was unveiled on the grounds of Confederation Building in St. John's, and the university campus at Corner Brook took his name after it opened in 1975.

Today, Grenfell's influence continues to loom very large on the Northern Peninsula and in parts of Labrador. But it is not without controversy. One of the most oft-repeated criticisms is that, in raising funds and bringing the world's attention to poverty and need in the area, Grenfell exaggerated a good deal and, in doing so, damaged both the image and the self-esteem of an independent-minded people. He is seen by some as a missionary of the old school, with all the paternalism and superiority that this implies.

But no final analysis of Grenfell can take him out of the context of the times in which he grew up and lived. He was, after all, an *avowed* zealot, unashamed of explaining all his work in terms of his calling by God. Whether he exaggerated or not, his flamboyance and single-mindedness were honed to a sole purpose of building and planning for the needs—medical, social, economic and spiritual—of the people he chose to serve. He is unlikely to be remembered kindly in the context of national or regional pride, and yet a paradox lies in the fact that he saw the dependence on the merchant and lack of financial independence as being one of the great evils facing the fishermen of his district. He is perhaps best summed up as a particularly robust example of the Victorian zeal for reform and charity carried fearlessly into the twentieth century.

CAPTAIN BOB BARTLETT

Photo credit: *The Log of Captain Bob Bartlett.*

The captain's face had the ruddiness born of years on cold Arctic waters, and his hands the calluses and scars that all seamen bear. His skin had the darkness of his Basque ancestors. His body was thick, his hair a shock of bearlike fur. Despite all this, there was absolutely no roughness about him.

Instead, Captain Robert Bartlett of Brigus, Newfoundland was gentle, making almost no noise as he moved about the galley of the *Karluk*. His movements were graceful—his touch had the softness of a rose petal.

Bartlett had already evacuated the crew as the *Karluk* began to sink into the Arctic Ocean; they were warming themselves in an igloo they had built on a nearby ice pan. Some of them visited him through the night, but he said little as he played his gramophone records and fed them into the fire.

Before she was trapped and then crushed in the ice, the *Karluk* had been the lead ship in Canadian explorer Vilhjalmur Stefansson's 1913–1918 scientific expedition. As she sank, the captain ordered his men to hoist the ensign; it would fly till the end. Then he played Chopin's "Funeral March" over and over.

Finally, at three fifteen in the afternoon, Bartlett announced "She's going!" Then, with the deck almost submerged, he put the "Funeral March" on the Victrola again. When the water came up to the rails, he stepped onto the ice wordlessly.

Though he is perhaps best known for leading Peary to the North Pole (or not—the jury is still out), Bartlett's most notable feat was yet to come. After the *Karluk* sank, he and Kataktovik, an Inuk, left the stranded crew at Wrangel Island, northwest of Siberia. Then they walked 700 miles over some of the roughest ice in the world to East Cape in the Bering Strait to get help.

Robert Abram Bartlett was born in the seafaring town of Brigus, Conception Bay in 1875. He came from a long and well-known line of skippers. He was the great-grandson of William "Follow On" Bartlett, the great sealing captain known for his daring feats. Captain William was said to have left Brigus to go seal hunting in an open boat, "following on" to Baccalieu, Cape Bonavista, the Funk Islands, and finally Spotted Islands off the coast of Labrador.

Captain Abram Bartlett, Robert's grandfather, commandeered the SS *Panther* for seventeen years. He imported miners from Cornwall, England to drill a large tunnel through a rock in Brigus, so his ship would have adequate mooring facilities. One hundred feet long, the tunnel is a popular site to visit today.

Robert's father, the darkly handsome William J., set a record for seal hunting in the Cabot Strait, bringing in over 440,000 pelts (an average of more than 10,000 a year). William J. also skippered the SS *Panther*, in which he rescued over 400 victims of the Labrador Disaster of October 1885, and brought them back to the safety of their Conception Bay homes.

Captain Samuel Bartlett, William's brother and Robert's uncle, also made his mark on the maritime world. Samuel skippered the steam yacht *Windward*, which took Peary to the Arctic in 1898. He also captained the *Neptune*, which made trips to the high north for the Canadian government. On the *Neptune*'s 1904 voyage, Ellesmere Island was claimed for King Edward VII.

His blood thick with the sea, Robert took charge of his first vessel at seventeen, fishing out of Turnavik, Labrador, where his grandfather had established a summer station. His association with Admiral Peary began not long after he got his master mariner's papers, at the age of twenty-three. He was first mate, under his uncle, Samuel, in the *Windward*. Although this trip was unsuccessful—Peary suffered frostbite and gangrene—Robert Bartlett had caught the bug for Arctic travel. From then on, his life would be all about northern voyages.

Peary was impressed with the young man, and asked him to accompany him on his Arctic journey—as skipper. They travelled in the *Roosevelt*, but the ship proved to be in bad condition; soon after Bartlett joined the ship in Cape Breton, two of her boilers exploded, leaving her with one. Somehow, though, they made it to Ellesmere Island, and, after more than 120 days of caching supplies and sledging toward the Pole, they came within 87°6'. With many of their dogs dead, they had to turn around.

The trip back to New York was almost disastrous, as one thing after another went wrong with the *Roosevelt*. At one point, the ship

CAPTAIN BOB BARTLETT'S AWARDS

- Hubbard Medal of the National Geographic Society
- United States Congressional Peary Polar Expedition Medal
- American Geographical Society Medal
- Kane Medal of the Geographical Society of Philadelphia
- Person of National Importance—Historic Sites and Monuments Board of Canada (posthumous)

struck rocks and lost her rudder, and Bartlett and his crew had to fashion another one.

Undeterred, Bartlett again sailed northward with Peary in 1908, also on the *Roosevelt*. The ship reached Cape Sheridan, and Bartlett took command of the first party to head to the Pole. Bartlett got within 150 miles of the Pole, and from then on the story gets murky. When Peary reached Bartlett's camp, he ordered the captain back to the ship. While Peary claimed he had reached the Pole (with his servant, Matt Henson, an African-American), there is a lasting debate about whether or not he did. Captain Bob Bartlett, however, believed him. When the *Roosevelt* returned to New York, both of them were given heroes' welcomes.

After World War I, Bartlett tried to raise funds for his own exploration trip to the Arctic. A friend bought him a 120-ton schooner, the *Effie M. Morrissey*, and he fitted her for the icebound waters of the North Atlantic and the Arctic Oceans. In western Greenland, he collected marine life, and he undertook two surveys of Foxe Basin. Bartlett even starred in a film, Varick Frissel's *The Viking* (1929). During World War II, he helped establish supply bases and weather stations for the United States military.

His northern trips were in the service of the American Museum of Natural History, the University of Michigan, the

Museum of the American Indian, the American Geographical Society, and the Smithsonian Institute.

In these ventures, we see Bartlett's tender side—the side that filled him out, that made him even more compelling. On his trips north, Bartlett lovingly collected alpine plants and wrote home about them in great detail. He was also a lover of wild flowers. This big, strong man, capable of the most daunting physical feats, and descended from a long line of daring sealing skippers, simply adored the tiniest, most beautiful little plants. Captain Bartlett was a connoisseur of classical music, a collector of the finest gramophone recordings of the day. He bought these on his frequent trips to New York City, where he eventually made his home.

He was as absorbed in these pursuits as he was in any of the dangerous icy adventures in which he regularly found himself. For that, he is wholly human, much more than a swashbuckler, much more than a character or a crusty old sea captain with a string of tales to tell. Instead, he embraced the silences and softnesses of life as well as its thunderous roars.

Captain Robert Bartlett died in New York City on April 28, 1946, after he contracted pneumonia. Hawthorne Cottage, his home in Brigus, which is open to the public in summers, is now a National Historic Site of Canada.

Visit Hawthorne Cottage at:
www.historicsites.ca/hawthorne.html

LETTER FROM CAPTAIN BOB BARTLETT
(From *Newfoundland Ships and Men*,
by Andrew Horwood, reprinted as written)

SS *Roosevelt*
Etale
North Vreenland (sic)
August 15, 1905

SIR,

Leaving Sydney 26th ult we had smooth water and fair wind. Midnight Saturday we landed the mails at Domino. Thick fog was encountered nearly all the distance over. We sighted the *Sukkertoppen* on the evening of the 3rd inst following the Greenland Coast Melville Bay was crossed in thirty-three hours on the 7th inst and Cape York was reached. Immediately we began picking Esquimaux and dogs.

Some of Peary's choice men were on some of the islands in Melville Bay which went on, going back thirty miles. Having secured them we reached North Star Bay where the *Erik* lay. On the morning of the 9th, Peary with the Esquimaux also to have a day or two hunting walrus for dog meat.

The *Roosevelt* immediately started for Etale so as to get ready for taking coals and having boilers and engines overhauled. The *Erik* arrived here on Sunday morning and Monday started to unload coal on the *Rosevelt* (sic). We shall take about one hundred and fifty tons coal and will leave for one trip through Smith Sound Rose Basin Etc. To-morrow evening.

The season has been early and warm. No ice has been seen until last Friday. From the high hills it appears close and heavy but water can be seen on the west side up as far as Sabine.

The Peary Arctic Club has offered twenty-five thousand dollars to be divided amongst the members of the crew should any one of the members of the crew reach the Pole and return in 1906.

Our Almy boilers are not working satisfactorily but we have them fitted up in shape now. Could we only keep up the steam I have no doubt of her steaming ten knots. Whilst going in North Star Bay, in keeping over to go alongside of the *Erik*, the ship grounded, the engines were stopped so had not much steam. The engineer let the steam come up to 180 lbs and she came off like a streak. Could we only hold that it would be fine; with our Almy boilers working I imagine we shall hold that pressure. It is a great pity she did not have another Scotch boiler about the same size as the one that is in her. Peary was advised by his friends alto against his own wishes to have Almy boilers. The idea was that in a push steam could quickly be raised and that also twenty-five tons of coal could be saved.

We are bringing with us 150 dogs, twenty Esquimaux and all their outfit. I sincerely hope we shall get the ship up to 85 degrees and if we do I am pretty sure Peary will reach the Pole.

Yours Faithfully
Robert A. Bartlett

NORTHERN NEWFOUNDLAND NURSE-MIDWIFE

MYRA BENNETT

Bennett House. © 1998 Heritage Foundation of Newfoundland and Labrador.

She was a nurse in London, England, planning to practice in Saskatchewan with the Imperial Overseas Nursing Association. The Canadian prairies needed nurses—she had read of a woman who had died in labour there—and she was the adventurous type. While she was waiting for her passage to be arranged, she met Lady Constance Harris, the wife of Alexander Harris, Governor of Newfoundland. Lady Harris had visited the outports in 1920, and concluded for herself that Newfoundland needed nurses, too, desperately, she insisted. Would Myra Grimsley consider it? They could offer her a two-year contract under the sponsorship of the Outport Nursing scheme, paying seventy-five dollars a month ($900 a year).

Grimsley thought about it and said yes, she would go to Newfoundland. And so began a story that lasted more than fifty years.

Myra Maud Grimsley was born to a working-class family in London in 1890. She worked for six years as a tailor before training as a nurse. After her general nurse's training, Grimsley went on for further, more specialized study. This included a six-month course in maternity work, three months of trial casework, and courses in operative midwifery and anaesthesia. Her general nursing had included dealing with the usual illnesses, often in emergency situations. But all along, her goal had been to deliver babies. So she did the extra courses, and succeeded in obtaining the coveted Central Midwives Board Certificate.

After graduating, she worked as a District Nurse in Woking, near London, as a caseworker in North London, and as a resident nurse in a London home for unwed mothers. For two years, she was head matron at a maternity hospital. Her work as a nurse in England lasted ten years, until she was thirty-one.

Grimsley's journey from London to Newfoundland in 1921 took six weeks, via Liverpool, from which she sailed. Three other English nurses accompanied her; they were stationed at Burgeo, Hant's Harbour, and Fogo Island. She was posted to Daniel's Harbour, a small fishing community on the western side of the Great Northern Peninsula. Grimsley's territory was the stretch of coastline from Sally's Cove in the south to Port au Choix in the north. She immediately became the only professional medical person on a coastline that stretched more than 200 miles; the nearest doctor was Dr. Fisher in Curling, well south of the community in which she lived.

At the time, there were no roads on the peninsula (Daniel's Harbour would not get a road connection until 1957). The primary mode of transportation that connected its communities to each other was a coastal steamer that operated in good weather.

Other than that, people travelled by small boat when harbours were ice-free, and by dog team and sled in winter. They were great walkers, too, and sometimes journeyed by horse. The nearest hospital was hundreds of miles away to the north at the Grenfell Mission in St. Anthony; in effect, it was not a facility of which most of the peninsula's people could easily avail. The cottage hospitals in Port Saunders, well north of Daniel's Harbour, and Norris Point, well south of it, would not open until 1938. The contrast to London could not have been greater, yet Grimsley took to the fresh air and open spaces. And she loved dogsledding.

During her first year in Daniel's Harbour, she married Angus Bennett, who had been in the merchant marines and then became a businessman. The next year, 1923, they moved into the two-storey house with four bay windows (two on each floor) Angus built in the middle of the village. The Bennetts were a family now, and Myra would not be going to Saskatchewan after all. They got a cow that Myra milked, they put in a kitchen garden, and began to have children: Grace; Barbara; and Trevor. Store-bought clothes were hard to get, so Myra made most of what they wore, and she made most of the bread they ate. Like most of the women in Daniel's Harbour, she was also involved in the local church. Like them, too, she sheared sheep, carded and spun wool, knitted, hooked mats, and made sealskin boots for her children.

But mostly, she was "the nurse." On the Great Northern Peninsula, her nursing career quickly became a legend, with the *Evening Telegram* giving her the epithet "the Florence Nightingale of Newfoundland." Myra Bennett delivered more than 500 babies, and extracted over 3,000 teeth. In her view, her greatest medical achievement came only five years after she first moved to the island. It happened when her brother- in-law Alex slipped and fell into the teeth of a lumber saw and almost severed his foot—it was attached only by a thin strip of flesh. Bennett cleaned the wound to the best of her ability, and then stitched Alex's foot back onto his leg. Then she and Angus bundled up Alex for the two-day trip to the doctor in Bonne Bay. According to the doctor, she had done such a good job that amputation was not necessary, and Alex was able to keep his foot.

Things did not always go this well for the outport nurse. One of the greatest challenges she faced was rough terrain with which she was unfamiliar. Travelling over streams, bogs and ponds took up so much of her time, and often she was in a race against the clock in trying to get to a patient. Only in winter was it relatively easy to cross water by dog team and sled, or horse and sleigh or on foot. One time, when Bennett was walking to see a patient, her foot went through thin ice and got caught at the heel by a submerged root. In the wrangling to get it loose, she broke a small bone in her instep. Finally, she got her foot out of the boot, a pliable skinboot, and then removed the footwear itself from its watery trap. Then she started again on her way to see her patient, albeit "somewhat lamely." She was tough, though, and always practical: "I recovered without too much pain and bother."

Another challenge was the general lack of medical knowledge among the population of the coast, especially when it came to tuberculosis. Infectious diseases were not generally well understood in those days, and Nurse Bennett had a difficult time persuading people that TB could easily be passed from one family member to another. Parents, siblings and other relatives all had the habit of sitting around the bed of the sick relative, and rarely could Bennett persuade them not to do this. Many people thought she was "TB crazy"; they didn't believe TB was catching, especially when not all family members fell ill. These were sad times. Tuberculosis raged all over the world, including Newfoundland, where the sanatoria at St. Anthony and St. John's were usually full, and expensive.

Finances were another ongoing issue in Bennett's life. When her contract with the Outport Nursing Association had expired, she was not replaced.

The provision of medical services had improved by that time, but the next available nurse was still thirty miles up the coast, at least a day's journey across a bay—impossible to reach in bad weather. So, for the next ten years, Bennett essentially had a private practice. She charged fifty cents for a house call, and roughly five dollars for a baby delivery. This worked out to about one dollar per hour, and perhaps ten to twenty cents per drug. The rate might increase if she had to travel a significant distance to the mother-to-be's home, or use forceps or sew stitches.

She never required payment, her son once told an interviewer, but if families could afford it, she expected them to pay. She knew many couldn't. She understood that the truck system, which she vocally deplored, meant that most were perennially short of cash. Many times Angus paid for the drugs himself and never complained, says Trevor Bennett. Presumably, he also got used to his wife performing minor surgery on the kitchen table.

Pregnant women were scattered all over the peninsula, so Bennett urged them to come to Daniel's Harbour and stay with relatives and friends when their due date came near. That way, she could leave no new mother untended. This new system raised the ire of some of the older midwives in the area, but Bennett persisted, and it stayed throughout her tenure.

In 1934, she had a steady income once again, when the Commission of Government put her on its payroll. Besides delivering her usual nursing and midwifery services, the Commission also charged her with providing midwifery courses to local women of her choice. She chose Freda Moss Guinchard (whose family she had stayed with when she first came to Newfoundland), Gertrude House, Elsie House, Prudence Guinchard and Sara House. She trained the women from January to June 1936, in a course she designed that was very hands-on, as well as theoretical. All the students passed their exams and were free to practice as midwives.

Bennett was unusual among Newfoundland midwives in that, as though she had never left the London hospitals from which she came, she kept meticulous records. Although she later estimated she had delivered 500 babies, she kept detailed records of only 343 obstetric cases from 1921 to 1955 (which is a large number indeed). These births differed significantly from those carried out by most of the traditional midwives known to rural Newfoundlanders elsewhere in the province during the same time period. Although no doctor was present and they did not take place in hospital, they were medicalized procedures. Bennett used drugs in sixty-five per cent of these births, mainly: ergot to help expel the placenta; morphine or Demerol to reduce pain; and chloral hydrate, a sedative to relieve anxiety and tension. With her hospital training, Bennett would have administered these drugs when she perceived the need, and would not have asked permission. This was standard practice at the time.

Bennett officially retired from nursing in 1953, although she always lent a hand whenever anyone was sick in the community or in neighbouring villages. She never really stopped being "the nurse." She died in 1990 at age 100. Her husband Angus died three years later at age ninety-six, leaving the Daniel's Harbour house he had built for them empty.

"I went where I wanted to go, and I stayed there because I was needed," Myra Bennett once explained her vocation in Northern Newfoundland. Her accomplishments there were much celebrated during her long lifetime. She was written about in *Reader's Digest,* and her biography was published as *Don't Have Your Baby in the Dory,* by H. Gordon Green. CBC-TV made a documentary about her life and exciting nursing career, called "Lady of the Lonely Places." From her native land, she was awarded the King George V Jubilee medal, the King George VI Coronation medal, and the Queen Elizabeth II Coronation medal. She was also made a Member of the British Empire, and inducted into the Order of Canada. Memorial University awarded her an honorary degree.

The home of Myra and Angus Bennett and their children was recognized as a Registered Heritage Structure in November 1991. It had changed little over the years, with only the addition, in 1942, of a separate clinic for Myra to work in. Bennett House had its grand opening on July 10, 1999, with 250 people in attendance. In its first season, 1,313 people visited the house, according to the Nurse Myra Bennett Foundation newsletter. Every summer, Bennett House continues to welcome visitors from around the world who are fascinated to learn the story of Nurse Bennett. On March 7, 2000, the

NURSE MYRA BENNETT FOUNDATION
PO Box 31
Daniel's Harbour
NL, A0K 2C0
709-243-2055/2601

Foundation received the Manning Award from the National Historic Sites and Monuments Board, for its work in preserving and presenting Newfoundland Heritage and involving the community in doing so.

Myra's story has also been brought to the stage. "Tempting Providence: The Nurse Myra Bennett Story" was written by playwright Robert Chafe. It was first performed in 2002 to sold-out audiences and standing ovations at the Gros Morne Theatre Festival in Cow Head. In April 2003, it was performed at the National Arts Centre in Ottawa. According to the *Ottawa Citizen* reviewer, the play was "wonderful" and "heartfelt." It has since been performed in several international locations, including Tasmania.

BIRTHING FOR GENERATIONS

TRADITIONAL NEWFOUNDLAND MIDWIVES

Photo credit: Resettlement Web site, Maritime History Archive, Memorial University of Newfoundland.

Most Newfoundland midwives lacked formal training of any kind. Marion Murphy was a midwife from Salmon Cove, Conception Bay. She was born into a family of thirteen on January 23, 1903. She had very little elementary schooling, because winter weather often made it difficult for the teacher to get to her community. Like most midwives, Marion served an apprenticeship with an older midwife. At the time of her apprenticeship, she was thirty years old and married. She would eventually have nine children of her own.

Murphy saw midwifery as a way to serve her community. She didn't do it for the money; she told writer Marian Frances White she got more respect than money! Sometimes she got five dollars for her services, which included cooking, cleaning, and caring for the mother's other children after the birth of her new baby, while at other times she was paid in kind. Murphy attended about 100 births, and all were healthy babies; there were no stillbirths, and her patients experienced no tearing.

Betty Picco was born in Portugal Cove, Conception Bay in 1866, to Susannah and Henry Miller. She became a widow very soon after her marriage, when her husband drowned. A woman in her circumstances had limited options in those days in rural Newfoundland, so she decided to become a midwife. She studied a medical book to add to her practical knowledge; this indicates that she must have had enough schooling to be literate. Like Murphy, Picco was often paid in kind. Like many traditional Newfoundland midwives, Picco provided a range of medical services besides midwifery. She was known as "Aunt Betty," and delivered 700 babies in her long career.

In those days, pregnant women rarely saw a physician. In 1923, there were only forty doctors off the Avalon Peninsula, while more than seventy per cent of Newfoundland's population was rural. Pregnant women saw the midwife about two months before their due date, and then received care from her for some weeks afterwards. Most traditional midwives used a combination of superstition and medicine to provide maternal care and bring babies into the world. Some placed an axe under the labour bed to relieve the pain of contractions.

> **A TRADITIONAL BELIEF**
>
> It was believed that a child born with a caul (a piece of amniotic sac) would become a healer. If the caul was preserved, it would prevent drowning. If hung on a string around the neck, it would prevent sickness.

Others gave expectant mothers senna tea made from leaves or pods to induce labour if the baby was late (this had the added benefit of cleaning the bowels). After childbirth, a midwife might give a new mother juice from boiled crowberries, to relieve uterine pains and to stop bleeding.

The tradition was that the new mother stayed in bed nine days after giving birth, while the midwife tended to her, cooked, cleaned, and minded her other children. There were wet nurses, too, when mothers could not give milk. An alternative was to grease the mother's breasts with butter, to bring on the milk. Men were never present during childbirth; they waited next door until someone came over and told them a baby was born.

Sometimes, midwives gave advice about contraception. Breast-feeding was thought to be effective, as was the use of sponges soaked in vinegar. At times, a midwife might advise a new mother to pass her child through the limbs of a dogberry tree, or any "apse" tree, to ensure its good health and make it immune to diseases like measles, smallpox and rickets.

Traditional midwives delivered many healthy babies in Newfoundland, but infant mortality rates were extremely high, as were maternal mortality rates. This was the case for most societies elsewhere at the time. After World War I, there was a push to improve health and welfare in Newfoundland, with the result that the Child Welfare Association was formed in 1921. The Outport Nursing Committee was

---

A SIGN OF THE TIMES

Dr. Samuel Carson (1803–1860), son of the politician William Carson, used chloroform, an anaesthetic, to relieve the pain of women in labour. He was charged with interfering with God's will as expressed in the Bible: "in sorrow thou shalt bring forth children." The charges were later dropped.

also formed—this was the or-ganization that sponsored nurse-midwives like Myra Grimsley Bennett from England.

In 1920, the Midwives Club was established, with Evelyn Cave Hiscock as president. Hiscock was a St. John's–born, Boston-educated nurse determined to standardize nursing and midwifery care across the island. The Midwives Club thus developed standards of care and held weekly classes. By 1925, sixty women had completed training and practiced with the guidelines of the Midwives Act of 1921. This signalled the decline of traditional midwifery in Newfoundland. It declined further with the establishment of the cottage hospital system in 1935. Most midwives in the cottage hospital system were British-educated nurse-midwives. By the 1960s, the construction of large hospitals in major centres throughout Newfoundland reduced the role of nurse-midwives. By the twenty-first century, midwives could not even practice in Newfoundland, although increasing numbers of women were beginning to agitate for a return to the personal, patient-centred care midwives had once provided here.

A MILLIONAIRE IN SEALS

CAPTAIN ABRAM KEAN

Photo credit: *Old and Young Ahead* (Flanker Press).

The world's largest flipper supper" took place on May 1, 1934, at Pitts Memorial Hall in St. John's. Given by the Methodist College Literary Institute, the dinner marked the "outstanding achievement" of Captain Abram Kean, of bringing to port over one million seals—1,052,737, to be exact. He had taken his millionth seal while skipper of the *Beothic* at age seventy-eight. The dinner speakers included Justice Higgins and Mayor Mews, and there was group singing under the direction of Gordon Christian. Kean had already gotten accolades from Bowrings and the St. John's Board of Trade. Best of all, his one millionth seal had made him a member of the Order of the British Empire (O.B.E.). May 1 was a glorious night for Newfoundland's most famous and successful seal killer.

Abram Kean was born on July 8, 1855, on Flower's Island, Bonavista Bay, the ninth[2] child of Joseph and Jane Kean. He began to distinguish himself early by becoming the first person on Flower's Island to attend school. To accomplish this, he had to leave; at eight, he packed up and went off to Pools Island, and then Greenspond.

The start of his education was memorable. Kean wrote that, as his father was about to leave him, he "broke down with homesickness and cried bitterly to go back again to Flowers Island, which I thought then was the most beautiful place on earth." Then, when Kean's new teacher appeared, he "told my father he ought to take a piece of rope and give me a whipping. As can be imagined, this beginning to my schooldays was anything but pleasant." Thus, Kean became the first literate native of Flower's Island. He had four years of schooling before he convinced his father to let him go fishing at thirteen.

His youth was difficult in other ways as well. He accidentally shot and killed his three-year-old nephew, and badly wounded his own hand. The incident "absolutely unnerved" him, and he could not return to his uncle's Pools Island home as a result. When he finished his schooling and was about to return home, he learned that his mother, whom he loved dearly, was dying.

Kean's childhood was over. By seventeen, he was married, to Caroline Yetman of Cape Freels, Bonavista Bay (his family's housekeeper, and seven years his senior). He fished and sealed, supporting his ill brother and various orphaned nieces and nephews. He shouldered his huge responsibilities matter-of-factly, but he was ambitious. By 1882, when he was twenty-seven, he was, in his own words, impatient and had no wish to serve any longer under another man. Baine Johnston accepted his application for the captaincy of the sealer *Hannie and Bennie*, and he was off to the ice.

---

2 Or tenth, depending on the source

The seal hunt occupies a prominent place in the Newfoundland psyche. Writer David Benson says that it was the seal hunt, not the migratory codfishery, that allowed the European settlers to live here year-round. This is certainly true of the icebound Northeast Coast. When the seal hunt became the focus of an international animal rights campaign in the 1970s, one result was a widespread knee-jerk Newfoundland nationalism. Many Newfoundlanders were hurt by attacks on our pride in ourselves as a tough, hardy people, however simplistic this view may be. Although it was mainly associated with the island's Northeast Coast, the seal hunt, to a large degree, became synonymous with Newfoundland, at least for a time.

Kean was the ultimate seal killer and, with his barrel chest and neat beard, looked the part. In November 1937, *Maclean's Magazine* wrote an article on him, saying that a top-notch sealing captain had to be "a combination of Al Capone, Admiral Byrd, and Sir Herbert Holt." When his first schooner sank, Kean and his crew made land in a dory and were later picked up by a passing ship. Never one to lick his wounds, he went home, repaired an old boat, and somehow hauled a record catch of cod, clearing all his debts.

The instinct for killing seals seemed to be bred deep within Kean's bones. Perhaps he had a distant Beothuk ancestor. One time, he sighted a large herd of seals way across the ice. With his crew, he walked nine miles over pack ice to get to them, reaching them at daylight. To make themselves light, the men shed their clothes to their underwear and surrounded the seals in a circle. Then they crept in toward the animals. When Kean gave the signal, by raising his cap on a pole, the men rushed in and the killing began. The ice was soon blood-red. They killed every seal—more than 2,000.

He continued to cut a swath through the ice every spring. Almost always the highliner, Kean had a record in 1910, when he returned to port with 49,069 pelts in the hold of the *Florizel*. The record stood for twenty-three years. Kean would go to the ice for sixty-three years, forty-eight as master. He was completely driven. The sealers knew him as "the Old Man." His friend, Sir Wilfred Grenfell, wrote of him as "the doyen of our ice hunters and northern seamen." Everyone had an opinion of him. This was even more true after the tragic *Newfoundland* disaster of 1914, one of two pivotal events in Kean's long life.

Kean was master of the *Stephano* for Bowrings that year, while his youngest son Westbury was skippering the *Newfoundland* for Harvey's. When a large number of Wes's men showed up at Kean's ship on their way to find seals, he gave them a mug-up, pointed them in the direction of a patch, and sent them on their way—in spite of signs of imminent bad weather. The party got lost, and was stuck on the ice for more than two days, while each captain thought they were safe on the other ship. Harvey's had removed the wireless from their vessels to save money. Seventy-eight men and boys died on the ice; many of the survivors were badly disabled and traumatized.

Two members of the inquiry that followed found Kean partially responsible for the tragedy. The third member said the *Newfoundland* disaster was an act of God. Although he was still lauded as the greatest seal killer ever, the Old Man's reputation was never the same after that. In the minds of many, he had hammered a nail in his own casket when he sailed into St. John's with all flags flying, in true highliner fashion, the spring of the *Newfoundland* disaster.

Kean did not accept any responsibility for what had happened on the ice in 1914. In 1934, he published his autobiography *Old and Young Ahead*[3], called after the familiar cry at the front. He wrote:

---

3 Re-released by Flanker Press in 2000 and still in print.

"Through no fault of my own I was subjected to the most bitter attack launched on any man in this or in any other country." He blamed William Coaker, who relentlessly attacked him in the pages of the *Mail and Advocate,* the newspaper of the Fishermen's Protective Union. Kean responded by suing Coaker for defamation of character. He won both cases.

Of his chief opponent, he reflected: "It is only fair to say that Coaker was perhaps deceived by many who had concocted vile stories about me. To my mind a man of his intelligence should have exercised better judgment than to have believed them." While he allowed that not all unionists were against him, he had harsh words for many: "...(they) have gone down to the vile dust from which they had sprung, unwept, unhonoured, and unsung." A deeply religious man, he wrote: "Others sought forgiveness on their deathbeds. I answered that they not only had my forgiveness but my sincere sympathy for being cajoled and fooled as they were." Kean devotes four pages of his autobiography to the campaign against him, but only a paragraph to the seal hunters who perished.

> Kean did not accept any responsibility for what had happened on the ice in 1914. He wrote: "Through no fault of my own I was subjected to the most bitter attack launched on any man in this or in any other country."

The incident may well have contributed to his electoral defeat in St. Barbe district on the Great Northern Peninsula in 1919. It was the first time he had lost an election. In fact, he had had a successful political career in the late 1800s. In 1885, he was elected as the Member of the House of Assembly for Bonavista for the Reform Party. In 1897, he ran for the Conservatives in Bay de Verde, and won with a large majority. The next year, he was appointed Acting Minister of Marine and Fisheries. Although the

> ## SOME MEMORABLE SEALING SPRINGS
>
> **The Spring of the Cats, 1832:** So called because of the large number of immature seals that were caught.
>
> **The Spring of the Wadhams, 1852:** More than forty vessels sealing near the Wadham Islands north of Fogo Island were caught in a gale and wrecked. More than 700 sealers were caught on the Wadhams from April 5, until they were rescued on April 12. Miraculously, few lives were lost.
>
> **The White Bay Spring, 1853:** Most seals that year were caught in White Bay. More than 180 vessels participated in the hunt.

ordinary voters on the Great Northern Peninsula didn't want Kean in the House after the *Newfoundland* disaster, he still had the support of the elites. In 1927, he was appointed to the Legislative Council, and served on it until it was dissolved in 1934.

The other central event in Kean's life was the unexpected death of his eldest son, Captain Joe, also a sealing skipper. Death was no stranger to Kean, but Joe's death filled him with grief. Joe was a passenger on the *Florizel* when she sank in a storm on the night of February 23, 1918, at Cappahayden some fifteen miles northeast of Cape Race[4]. In his autobiography, Kean wrote: "On hearing the news my feelings can be better imagined than described.... The funeral was beyond all doubt the largest ever seen in Newfoundland; it was not only impressive, it was heart-rending. I looked at it from every angle, but insurmountable difficulties seemed to be blocking the way. One thing I could not afford to do:

---

4 The story is told in *A Winter's Tale: The Wreck of the Florizel*, by Cassie Brown, re-issued by Flanker Press, 2003.

I could not afford to be a coward." The next day, he sailed for the front.

Above all, Abram Kean was motivated by duty—to family, country and King. He even saw killing seals as a service to his homeland, since it was an economic activity that contributed to the Newfoundland treasury. He explained his ethic in the conclusion to *Old and Young Ahead*: "My narrative...represents a sincere and careful account of fifty years in the service of my country."

A Methodist, a teetotaller and a monarchist, Kean was also a sometime Justice of the Peace in Labrador. Of sentencing an Inuit man at Hebron he wrote: "The laws and constitution of the English Government are the best in the world because they are nearest to the laws God has established in our natures. Those who have attempted this barbarous violation of the most sacred rights of their country deserve the name of rebels and traitors, since they not only have violated the laws of their King and country but the laws of Heaven itself." Although views of "the millionaire in seals" may seem alien at best to the modern reader, they were likely quite representative of his religion and social class at the time in Newfoundland, and give us great insight into a Newfoundland that has all but disappeared.

THE GRAND DAMES OF NEWFOUNDLAND POLITICS

ARMINE NUTTING GOSLING was born into genteel poverty in Waterloo, Quebec in 1863. At age twenty-one, she left her homeland to teach at the Church of England Girls' School in St. John's, which would later become Bishop Spencer College, with her as its principal. In St. John's, she met and married William Gilbert Gosling, a native of Bermuda who had moved to Newfoundland to work with Harvey and Company. William Gosling became very active in the Newfoundland Historical Society, and later was mayor of St. John's.

Armine Gosling immersed herself in the life of the city, always working in concert with other women. In 1904, she and a group of women raised $5,600 to rebuild the Anglican Cathedral, which had been badly damaged in the 1892 fire. She publicly noted the feminist contradiction inherent in doing this, remarking that women were loyally supporting "an institution that encourages us to work and takes with eagerness all the money we can earn, but denies us any voice in its expenditure, and relegates us to outer darkness as far as having any share in formulating its policies is concerned."

Gosling was right at the centre of the women's suffrage movement. She was probably its chief strategist in Newfoundland. She once said, "It is just as important to convince the public that women are angry as it is to convince them that women are right." Gosling and her female colleagues first attempted to get the vote for women in the 1890s, and then again in the years following, just prior to the First World War, but both attempts failed. One of their mistakes might have been the movement's focus on St. John's.

The suffragettes were more successful after World War I. Gosling, Margaret Duley, Fannie McNeil, and other women lobbied City Council hard and, in 1921, Mayor Gilbert Gosling granted the right to vote to women with the required amount of property (the franchise extended only to male property owners as well). In 1925, three women ran in the city elections—May Goodridge, Fannie McNeil, and Julia Salter Earle—but all were defeated. Goodridge and McNeil ran for the Women's party, of which Gosling was president.

> "It is just as important to convince the public that women are angry as it is to convince them that women are right."
> Armine Gosling defending the Newfoundland suffragettes

Armine Gosling and the other suffragettes now knew that the key to success was to extend their campaign across the island, and this became their strategy. Gosling put her talents as a gifted speaker and writer to work. Eventually, hundreds of Newfoundland women were involved with the cause. Women in every electoral district collected petitions and wrote letters. Finally, the government of Prime Minister Walter Monroe gave in and introduced legislation to give women the right to vote—women over twenty-five, that is. Men could vote at twenty-one.

Although her husband became a wealthy businessman, Gosling never forgot the grinding poverty of her own childhood in Quebec.

She believed that social and economic conditions for women and children would change only when women could vote and hold elected office. She also knew that the women's franchise would not mean automatic change for the better. So she tried to influence and change public policy.

With her husband, Gosling tried to improve health care by making sure nurses were available to the people of St. John's. With Gosling on its executive, the Women's Patriotic Association raised funds to pay nurses' salaries when the government would not. They canvassed door-to-door and collected several large private donations, making over $6,000 by mid-1919. This allowed them to pay the nurses' salaries, establish milk stations, and distribute clothing to families who needed it.

The next year, the Women's Patriotic Association opened a small children's hospital, but this closed a few months later, due to lack of funds. However, the women had impressed government with their dedication and ambition, or perhaps they had shamed the men in the Colonial Building. Not long afterwards, the government opened a children's ward in the General Hospital.

When Gilbert Gosling died in 1930, his wife Armine presented the 1,800 books in his personal library to the City of St. John's, to form the basis of a public library. It was opened in 1935 as the Gosling Memorial Library, but is now closed.

FRANCES KNOWLING MCNEIL, born in St. John's in March 1869, was the daughter of George Knowling and Elizabeth Upham. George Knowling came to St. John's from Exeter, England via a circuitous route that involved New Brunswick and Upper and Lower Canada. In Newfoundland, he served on St. John's City Council, and, in 1894, when Frances (or Fannie, as she was better known) was a young woman, he

Photo credit: Centre for Newfoundland Studies (William Knowling Collection).

was appointed to the Legislative Council, and then to cabinet as government leader under Sir Robert Bond. Politics, it seemed, ran in Fannie's blood.

After completing her education, Fannie married Hector McNeil, who was an accountant. She became an early member of the Ladies Reading Room and Current Events Club, the purpose of which was to allow city women to become more well-versed in issues and causes, local, national, and international. Fannie served on the club's executive, and later became its president.

It was inevitable that the Ladies Reading Room and Current Events Club would embrace the vote for women as a cause. Women's suffrage was a cause in England, where the Pankhursts women who led the movement were regularly arrested for their rowdy and "unladylike" behaviour. Attempts at gaining the vote for women had already been tried in Newfoundland in the 1890s. The time seemed ripe after World War I, when change was in the air and people wanted to turn a new page after the horrors of the trenches.

McNeil became one of the leaders of the struggle in Newfoundland. In 1920, she became the first secretary of the Women's Franchise League. A skilled organizer, she arranged public meetings and guest lectures, lobbied politicians, and circulated petitions throughout the island. She was not shy, and did not hesitate to participate in debates—anything to promote this just cause. A high point of the campaign was the presentation of a petition containing 20,000 signatures to the Newfoundland government. This was difficult to ignore.

Like Armine Gosling, McNeil had interests in other causes. She was a founding president of the Newfoundland Society of Art, which promoted local artists by arranging exhibits of their work in Newfoundland and elsewhere. The Society also brought in exhibits from other places, particularly of Newfoundland artists who lived away.

An unsuccessful city council candidate for the Women's Party in 1925, McNeil died three years later. In 1942, her fellow suffragettes honoured her by establishing the Hector and Fannie McNeil Memorial Trust Fund Scholarship at Memorial University, established in 1942.

Photo credit: Library and Archives Canada.

LADY HELENA EMILINE STRONG SQUIRES was cut from a different cloth than Gosling and McNeil. In fact, she was on the other side of the women's suffrage debate, being a strong opponent of the vote for women. In this, she stood side by side with her husband, Sir Richard Anderson Squires, the Prime Minister of Newfoundland. Yet, when the dust settled, Lady Helena became the first women elected to the Newfoundland legislature.

Helena Squires was born a twin in Little Bay Islands in 1879, the daughter of Ann Murchell and her merchant husband, James Strong. The Strongs were a wealthy family; their firm supplied the local shore fishery and voyages to the French Shore. After the 1894 Bank

Crash, they reorganized as Strong and Murchell, and expanded into the Labrador fishery, unlike many firms which had gone bankrupt at this time. Strong supplied as many as fifty schooners.

Squires was educated at the Methodist College in St. John's, and later at Mount Allison University in New Brunswick, where she was educated as a teacher. She studied elocution and public speaking at the Emerson College of Oratory in Boston, training that would later stand her in good stead in her political life. She also took a course at Harvard University Summer School, and studied Domestic Science at the Farmer Cooking School, as well as interior decorating while in New York. Hers was an unusual and privileged education for an outport woman in the late 1800s.

Squires did not support the Women's Franchise League and their cause. Perhaps, like her husband, she believed that the vote for women was unnecessary and unnatural. Or, she may just have been in an awkward position, married to a prime minister who was adamantly opposed to extending the franchise to women. During Prime Minister Squires's first term in office from 1919 to 1923, the suffragettes had no success and had to deal with constant frustration.

At some point, Helena must have changed her mind about women and politics. Five years after women were granted the right to vote by Prime Minister Monroe's government, Lady Helena Squires ran in a by-election in Lewisporte, necessitated by the death of MHA George Grimes. She was elected, becoming the first female MHA in Newfoundland's history. As an MHA, she was very popular on both sides of the House: she was intelligent, witty and well read. But her time in office did not last long;

As an MHA, Lady Helena Squires was very popular on both sides of the House; she was intelligent, witty and well read.

when she ran again for the Liberals in Twillingate in 1932, she was defeated.

Like Gosling and McNeil, Squires's civic involvements extended beyond politics. She, too, was interested in improving child welfare and public health, two pressing issues during the 1920s and the Great Depression. For many years, she was president of the Grace Hospital Auxiliary. Her last role in politics was in 1949, when she was elected the first president of the Liberal Association of Newfoundland. She died ten years later.

ST. JOHN'S ACTIVIST JULIA SALTER EARLE

Julia Salter Earle's home. Photo credit: Garry Cranford.

One day, at the height of the Great Depression, a petite woman led a march of 500 unemployed men through the streets of St. John's. They headed to the Colonial Building, the seat of the Newfoundland government, and were about to enter the building, when the tiny woman stopped and raised her hand.

"If you have liquor in your pockets, get rid of it," she said.

To a man, they obeyed her, and it was said liquor flowed down between the cobblestones of Colonial Street that day. The march was a successful one; the Commission of Government gave the men jobs crushing stones by hand for road gravel. It was not the most rewarding work, but at least it was work when work was almost impossible to come by.

Julia Salter was born in St. John's on September 20, 1878, the twelfth child of Elizabeth Brown Chauncey and William Thomas Hall Salter. She was educated at the Methodist College in the city. At age twenty-four, she married Water Street jeweller Arthur Edward Earle and together they had six children: daughters, End, Avis, and Edith, and sons, Alton, Horace, and Arthur.

For thirty-five years, Salter Earle worked as engrossing clerk for the House of Assembly, preparing for final endorsement by hand every law passed in the legislature. At the time, this was considered to be a very important job, and Salter Earle did it even through her married and child-rearing years, which was unusual for the time. Even when she was sick in bed, papers were brought to her. There, pillows were propped up behind her so she could write the laws in her beautiful script on special parchment paper. Because she wrote each of the laws by hand, she knew them well, and was often called upon to settle legal disputes.

It was as an activist, though, that Salter Earle really made her mark. She was on the fringes of the women's suffrage movement, but she refrained from joining fully in it, thinking it elitist (it was led by the city's aristocrats) and feeling that bread-and-butter issues were more pressing. Although her own background was relatively privileged, Salter Earle was drawn to the fight for workers' rights and the struggle against joblessness and poverty. She was instrumental in founding the Ladies Branch of the Newfoundland Industrial Workers Association (N.I.W.A.), of which she became president. In this capacity, Salter Earle brought poor wages and working conditions for working women to public attention; these were issues that had been entirely ignored in Newfoundland until she came along.

She frequently got involved in individual cases of injustice and hardship. One time, the family of a young woman injured at factory work called on Salter Earle for help. The family wasn't able to pay for the woman's hospitalization, so the word "pauper" was displayed above her bed on the hospital ward. Salter Earle called the firm's manager and directed him to page ninety-three of the book that outlined labour laws and standards. The manager saw that the firm was responsible for the injured worker's medical bills, and these were promptly paid. Salter Earle then suggested to the manager that he send the young woman some flowers and chocolates on behalf of the firm. These, too, were soon delivered.

Salter Earle made history at least twice. She became the first woman to lead a parade through the city of St. John's in 1921, when she headed the St. George's Day parade. Then, in 1925, after women finally won the right to vote, she ran for City Council. She was not the only woman on the ballot; Mae Kennedy and Fannie McNeil also stood for election. Salter Earle was a candidate for the local Labour Party, with the memorable slogan, "Vote for Julia, she won't fool you!"

She came within a hair's breadth of winning the sixth and final seat on Council—eleven votes. In fact, many people thought she did win it, especially after a ballot box went missing and wasn't located until the day after the election in a polling booth on Hayward Avenue. Salter Earle's supporters agitated for a recount, but the request for one had to come from the candidate

> Julia came within a hair's breadth of winning the sixth and final seat on Council—eleven votes. In fact, many people thought she did win it, especially after a ballot box went missing...

herself. For some reason, Julia Salter Earle did not ask for one, and she never again got involved in politics.

Her activism never waned, though. Her children recalled how there was often someone at the family door seeking their mother's help. She frequently took food right off the kitchen table and gave it to any callers who needed it. Julia's motivating force seemed to be: "I was hungry and ye fed me not," according to Eleanor McKim in 1965.

Salter Earle was strong-willed, her granddaughter Carol Earle told the *Telegram* in 1985, but also very sensitive. "She could easily be brought to tears if 'the wrong thing was said to her.'"

Salter Earle's death in 1945 was sudden, brought on, her doctors said, by heartbreak after one of her sons was killed overseas during the war. Her spirit seemed to live on, though; as late as fifteen years after her death, her son Alton continued to get phone calls and visits from people seeking his mother's assistance.

REBEL WITH A CAUSE

PEARCE POWER

He was something else. He held us spellbound." That was how one St. John's man remembered Pearce Power, labour leader, rabble-rouser, orator, convicted criminal, and the hope of Newfoundland's unemployed during the Dirty Thirties. Power preached the classic left-wing message: the injustice of the rich living off the work of the many. The *Telegram* considered him a contender for Newfoundlander of the millennium.

The Colonial Building during the riot of 1932. Photo credit: Provincial Archives of Newfoundland and Labrador.

Born on August 21, 1910, to Catherine Butler and Patrick Power, Pearce (sometimes the name is spelled Pierce) grew up on the capital city's Southside Road. He was a student at Holy Cross School, where he was a keen debater and showed an early talent for public speaking.

As a young man, Power travelled widely, mixing with socialists, trade unionists, and Marxist-Leninists. In his early twenties, he addressed a meeting of 25,000 unemployed people on Glasgow Green in Scotland. He crossed the North American continent under the name Patrick Joseph Murphy. Everywhere he went, he spread the message of the oppression of the masses, whom he encouraged to overthrow their masters. He lived for a time in Vancouver, B.C. until the Canadian government deported him for being "an agitator."

The 1920s and '30s were hard times, but they were heady times, too. The Russian Revolution was entrenched now, giving hope to Marxists all over the world, and inspiring fear among the rich. In North America, the anti-colonial Mexican Revolution had led to the redistribution of land to the people. In New York, the artist Diego Rivera caused an international sensation when he painted the face of Lenin into a mural he was commissioned to do in Rockefeller Centre; the Rockefellers protested, Rivera would not remove the detail, and the Rockefellers cancelled his contract. Meanwhile, Leon Trotsky, the brains of the Russian Revolution, established an organization called the Fourth International (see textbox).

Well read, Power would have been aware of all these developments, and they would have given him reason to think that the workers' revolution predicted by Karl Marx was at hand. He wrote: "It is now between the dictators and the masses of toiling Newfoundlanders trying to exist in their own country as decent human beings, a contest for right, justice and liberty between the proletariat and the oligarchy (Commission of Government) sent across the Atlantic to rule us against our will."

In 1934, Power helped form a marine firemen's union in the city. In the same year, he became involved with the Unemployed Committee. In turn, this organization became the Avalon Workers Protective Association (A.W.P.A.). In August 1934, Power was elected its chairman at a rally of 2,000 people, held at Parade Grounds, ironically now the site of Royal Newfoundland Constabulary Headquarters. He remained as chair for two years, regularly organizing rallies, protests and marches. His goal was to have branches throughout the island, and under his leadership the Association raised funds to that end. To publicize their goal and aims, the Association produced *The Avalon Workers Protective Association Bulletin,* which sold for two cents a copy.

The Commission of Government, which Power loathed, was his main target. He labelled the Commissioners indifferent to the suffering of Newfoundlanders thrown out of work by the Depression; because of their affluence, they were impervious to the effects of the worldwide economic downturn. In Power's view, they were uncaring, callous, typical of the class to which they belonged. *The Avalon Workers Protective Association Bulletin* proclaimed that the Commissioners said Newfoundlanders were too lazy to work. In turn, the Commissioners branded him a Communist and an agitator, not an original charge, but a tried and true formula when a government is trying to alienate an agent of change.

Power pressed the Commission to increase the dole (which was famously only six cents a day), pay rents for the destitute, create a public works scheme, and bring in a clothing allowance. He usually spoke at outdoor meetings, on Yellowbelly Corner at George Street and Water Street, the courthouse steps, or Beck's Cove. Crowds, unemployed and otherwise, inevitably gathered around him.

These outdoor scenes must have looked threatening to the powers-that-were, and must have given Power a certain aura of authority. The Commission of Government directed the Newfoundland Constabulary to watch Power and his associates closely. A network of informers called "One X" reported directly to the chief of police. Meanwhile, police officers themselves attended every rally and demonstration, taking notes of Power's speeches.

In response, Power stated publicly that the A.W.P.A. would operate only within the law. Otherwise, he said, its members would give the forces of law and order an excuse to curtail their worthwhile activities.

The year 1935 turned out to be the deciding one in Power's career. He might have hoped it would be the year revolution came to Newfoundland—he told a May Day rally, "Unless the working men have money to spend, there will be fun, and it will not be a singsong." The authorities seemed to have taken these as fighting words, as things turned out.

> **Power told a May Day rally, "Unless the working men have money to spend, there will be fun, and it will not be a singsong."**

All that spring, Power issued challenges, as if he were itching for a fight. In March, as the seal hunt was about to begin, he and his fellow socialist Joseph Smallwood spoke passionately to a sealers' meeting at the Majestic Theatre in downtown St. John's. The two men attacked the powerful Water Street merchants and their partners in crime, the Commission of Government[5]. Power urged the sealers to organize on their vessels, and then to strike for better working conditions and more money. He said, "What's needed is for you to take a determined stand. I'll guarantee the working class and the unemployed in the city will mobilize behind you."

Power waved a red flag in front of the Commission of Government on May Day that year when he spoke in front of 2,000 people in Beck's Cove. He pledged that he would get the Commission to recognize the A.W.P.A. as the official representative organization of the unemployed in Newfoundland. In this capacity,

---

5 Oddly, Power does not appear in Smallwood's comprehensive *Encyclopedia of Newfoundland and Labrador*.

Power promised, the unemployed would have control over public relief schemes, including the final say on who would work on these schemes. Given that there was not even an elected legislature in Newfoundland at this time, the likelihood of such a concession from the Commission was nil. It is hard to believe that Power did not know this. But he was a young man—not yet twenty-five—and perhaps hankering for a showdown with his enemies.

Ten days later, with Power's words ringing in their ears, approximately 400 men met again at Beck's Cove, St. John's. There, Power and his colleagues, George Wilkinson, Herbert Saunders and Joseph Milley, told the crowd they had done everything possible to get official recognition as a committee and could go no further. Power and Milley draped the Union Jack across their shoulders and led a parade up Water Street, Cochrane Street and Military Road to the Colonial Building, the seat of government.

A small number of police officers were there and ordered the crowd to move away from the Colonial Building (no doubt the memory of the 1932 riot was fresh in their minds). Instead, there were cries of "No!" and "We're going in!" Someone threw a stone. Suddenly, more than 100 members of the Newfoundland Constabulary materialized. Their numbers included Power's own brother, Mike, a constable. The black-clad cops carried billyknockers and, in those days, were hired for their bulk. In no time, blows rained down on the unemployed men as they approached the building.

The brawl lasted half an hour. Power

> **Avalon Workers Protective Association (A.W.P.A.) Executive Members**
>
> - Pearce Power
> - George Wilkinson
> - Herbert Saunders
> - John Cadwell
> - Joseph Milley

himself was injured, and had to be carried home to the Southside. Wilkinson got severe cracks on the head and was arrested but then let go because of his head wounds. Other men, including Milley, suffered head wounds that they got dressed at nearby Peddigrew's Drug Store. J.T. Meaney, a foreign journalist, got a minor leg wound. Four police officers were injured. The camera of the *Evening Telegram*'s staff photographer was smashed.

Angry and fed up, 800 men met that night on George Street and went on a rampage along Water Street West. They were without their leader, for Power was at home, ailing. Wilkinson was there, and he urged them not to be violent, but they ignored him. They damaged and looted a number of stores (fourteen, according to the *Daily News*, twenty according to the *Evening Telegram*). In addition, there was a great deal of stone-throwing at the police.

THE TROTSKY CONNECTION

Leon Trotsky, the Russian revolutionary figure, visited Newfoundland in or around 1936. On the run from Lenin, he was on his way to exile in Mexico. In Mexico City, he stayed with artists Diego Rivero and Frida Kahlo. He would die in 1937 after being attacked with an ice axe.

In St. John's, Trotsky stayed at the Cochrane Hotel, on Cochrane Street, named after Newfoundland's one-time Governor. Power may have been in jail when Trotsky passed through, but it is not difficult to imagine the two of them sharing a glass of ale and discussing the revolution into the wee hours of the night. Trotsky might also have met Wilkinson, Saunders and Milley, who would have told him about their ill-fated May 10, 1935, march, as well as the 1932 riot at the Colonial Building. Like the Avalon Workers Protective Association, Trotsky would have despised the Commission of Government and urged the unemployed to take matters into their own hands.

Only steel helmets saved them. Power's plan, if he had one, seems to have gone terribly awry, and the movement of the unemployed was discredited by the emotions that ran high that night, at least in the eyes of some.

Five men were arrested that night. Not surprisingly, Power was arrested at his home the next day. He and his colleagues stood trial for "unlawfully and riotously assembling together against the person of our lord the King, his crown and dignity." At first, it didn't look good for him. The *Evening Telegram* seemed to capture the mood of the day when it opined, "(the) law must be upheld...lawlessness and disorder is injurious rather than helpful to a cause." But this was the Great Depression, and there was some sympathy for the hordes of jobless men. With his public speaking talents and keen intelligence, Power successfully acted as his own lawyer, and all the accused were found not guilty.

After his amazing feat in court, things went horribly wrong for Power and, sadly for him and the unemployed people he represented, he was never able to fulfill the promise he so brilliantly displayed. On Christmas night in 1936, while apparently drunk, he got into a fight with neighbours on the Southside Road, where he still lived with his father. When a police officer responded to a call for help, Power attacked him, slashing his face, arms, and wrists with a straight-edged razor. The cop ended up spending almost a month in hospital.

This time, there was no disputing Power's guilt. He was convicted and spent a full five years in prison. He carried his activism into the jail cell, going on a hunger strike to protest bad food, overcrowding, and rough treatment at the hands of prison guards. With the help of his friend Anthony Ryall, he smuggled out a protest letter, which was published in the *Evening Telegram*.

Power tasted freedom again on Christmas Eve, 1940, during World War II. He joined the merchant marines, becoming a fireman in ships' engine rooms. He died less than a year later, on July 27, 1941. His ship, the SS *Kellwyn*, was torpedoed on her way from Scotland to Portugal with a load of coal. At the time of his death, Power was not yet thirty-two.

THE NIGHTINGALE OF THE NORTH

MARIE TOULINGUET

Photo credit: Centre for Newfoundland Studies.

A voice such as hers," enthused the *Boston Globe* in 1897, "one hears only once in a lifetime." The journalist was referring to Mademoiselle Marie Toulinguet, who, at the time of the review, was nearing the very peak of her career. With her effortless soprano—at once softly expressive, yet clear and powerful—it must have seemed as though the singer had been groomed from birth for the great opera houses, like Milan's La Scala, where she had already performed.

But Georgina Stirling—as Marie Toulinguet was baptized—was born and raised on North Twillingate Island on Newfoundland's rugged northeast coast. In a career that would soar to the dizzying heights of fame and then plummet to despair and near-destitution,

Twillingate remained the focal point, the place from which she came and would ultimately return.

The stage name Marie Toulinguet perfectly conveys a personality at once drawn to her home yet ambitious to travel far beyond its limiting shores. Toulinguet was the French name for Twillingate, in use before the 1713 Treaty of Utrecht curtailed French rights in Newfoundland. Georgina chose Marie, the French version of Mary, because the Twillingate islands were in Notre Dame Bay (literally the bay of "Our Lady").

Georgina, or Georgie as she was affectionately known by family and friends, was born on April 3, 1867, into an Anglo-Irish family of high standing in the Twillingate area. Her father, William Stirling, was one of a long line of doctors. Her mother, Ann, was daughter of the famous magistrate John Peyton Jr., whose home had once played host to the legendary Beothuk woman Shanawdithit.

The Stirling household, which boasted seven daughters, was both well-to-do and gregarious. The many musical evenings hosted by the Stirlings helped Georgina develop her abilities from an early age. And since the Stirlings were active in church and charity work, Georgie soon had many opportunities to show her early musical promise outside the home, playing organ in church or piano at charity functions.

But when Georgie was fifteen years old, this social idyll was shattered by her mother's death. The following year, William sent his younger daughters to boarding schools, while he undertook an extended tour of Canada and the United States.

William placed Georgina in the Toronto Ladies' College. This was more a "finishing school" than an academic institution, and it is likely that Georgina's musical abilities were considered desirable accomplishments in a young lady and nurtured.

Two years later, Georgina returned home to enliven the Twillingate social scene again with her singing and playing. Never abandoning the charity work for which the Stirlings were known, she also helped found the Dorcas Society, a religious organization that sewed clothes for the "industrious poor." But Georgina's involvement in such things would not last long. Impressed by her growing local reputation as a singer, her father took an audacious step. William decided that Georgie should go to Paris and study voice.

On October 27, 1888, Georgina sailed from the rugged shores of North Twillingate Island to St. John's, and thence to Liverpool. By late fall, she was wandering the lively boulevards of Paris, with their constant Renoir bustle and tall deciduous trees in full autumn colours. She took daily lessons with Madame Malthide Marchesi, a world-renowned mentor whose school was at the very centre of Parisian musical society. Madame Marchesi was personally acquainted with many of the great composers of the day, including Liszt and Massenet, and held soirees at which the great opera impresarios of Europe selected promising new talent.

At one of these events, in May 1890, Georgina was plucked to sing in Milan, and her ascendency in opera began in earnest. For the next few years, she shuffled between tours and engagements, which would last a few months, and Paris, where she would once again take lessons from Madame Marchesi.

In the summer of 1895, she returned in triumph to holiday in Newfoundland, where she wowed audiences in St. John's at a special concert, for the first time receiving the accolade "Newfoundland's Nightingale."

Although she was in steady employment in the opera, it wasn't until 1896 that Georgina achieved the status of lead performer, taking up with the Imperial Opera Company in New York. Her debut in October was a major success and turning point. "Her voice is of tremendous power with a sympathetic quality that fairly thrills," remarked the *New York Reporter*.

During all this public drama, Georgie's private life remained so much in the background that no record of a genuine romance

> And then, at the very pinnacle of her career, a short while after a famous performance in Chioggia, Italy, at which she had been honoured with delirious ovations and flowered bouquets which released doves and canaries into the auditorium, something went wrong.

has ever been found. The closest thing to a dalliance involved a young Newfoundland lawyer, who pursued her during one of her visits home with an ardour he presumably thought appropriate for a prima donna. In reply to his continued protestations, Georgie is reported to have looked at him and said, "And what would I do with you, young man?" The question seems fittingly haughty, yet also entirely practical.

However mysterious her private life, over the five years from 1896 to 1901, the accolades in both America and Europe increased until they reached the ultimate superlative—she was the greatest soprano in the world. And then at the very pinnacle of her career, a short while after a famous performance in Chioggia, Italy, at which she had been honoured with delirious ovations and flowered bouquets which released doves and canaries into the auditorium, something went wrong. Georgina's singing engagements came to a sudden pause. She stopped answering her friends' letters. The only two-way correspondence she had was with her worried sisters, Lucy and Janet, who lived in England. These communications referred euphemistically to some "trouble."

The panic and secrecy was not inappropriate. The worst fear for an opera singer had just come true. Marie Toulinguet had lost full control of her voice. The precise diagnosis—whether nodules or neuritis—and why she never recovered remains a mystery. But the enormous psychological trauma on her sensitive and optimistic nature sent Georgina into an irreversible decline. Very soon in financial straits, she went to London to live with Lucy and Janet.

As the months passed with no improvement in her voice, the three sisters set up public performances, and Georgie appeared as a concert artist, singing less-demanding songs which might disguise her diminished powers.

In 1904, Georgina returned again to Newfoundland for an extended holiday. So successful had the sisters been in keeping Georgie's voice affliction a secret that the newspapers proudly announced that she was returning with fresh laurels after new successful opera tours of Europe. In fact, she had done nothing in that line for three years.

And worse was to follow. On October 24, 1904, there was to be a Grand Recital in St. John's before Georgina's return to England. As her reputation in St. John's was undiminished, a huge crowd filled the hall where she was to appear. Precise accounts of what happened are sketchy, but Georgie apparently got so far as to step onto the stage. But she did not sing. The concert was postponed, and the following day the newspapers referred to a "slight indisposition."

It's quite possible this was the first evidence of a new secret affliction from which Georgina was beginning to suffer, one that helped her through depression and nerves, but at a cost. Georgie had begun to drink.

In the short term, Georgina's reputation in Newfoundland was reprieved, and she gave two well-received concerts before returning to England. But her sisters, who had by now become used to protecting the secrets of Georgie's failing career, thought steps had to be taken. Janet persuaded Georgie to join the Duxhurst Farm Colony for Women and Children in Surrey. There, patients—all woman with drinking problems—cultivated and harvested food. The hope was that being close to the cycles of nature would help them to heal.

Georgie seemed to thrive in this environment, and it was here she stayed, even through World War I. When finally her sister, Janet, who was now her sole support, died in 1928, arrangements were made between a lawyer and another sibling in the U.S. to transport the now solitary and near-destitute Georgina back to Twillingate.

It must have been a tortuous journey for the sixty-two-year-old. Coming through the narrows into St. John's Harbour, with its painful recollections of triumphant returns long past, Georgina must have felt the cruellest of contrasts. After the long train and steamship journey to Twillingate was over, she was reunited with her elderly sister, Rose, and the old family home, which was a desolate ghost of its former elegant self.

But, soon it became clear that Georgie's varied career had given her resources undreamed of before. In a short while, she cultivated a famously beautiful garden—skills no doubt learned at the farm colony—and old acquaintances were said to have innocently remarked that Georgina had given up on singing and instead taken up horticulture. Georgie also put a great deal of her energy in her final days into the Dorcas Society she had helped form all those years ago.

When she died on April 23, 1935, she was known no longer as a great star, but as a respected elder of Twillingate society with a remarkable and glamorous past.

Sadly, the only recording of Marie Toulinguet was made in 1904, after her great voice was damaged. Yet the contemporary descriptions of her voice live on—infinitely expressive, yet clear and powerful.

And there's one other reminder of how events out of living memory can be rediscovered. Georgina's body lay in an

> In 1983, Amy Louise Peyton wrote the loving biography *Nightingale of the North* (Jesperson Publishing), paying tribute to Georgina's life and achievements.

unmarked grave in Snelling's Cove cemetery for almost thirty years after her death. In 1964, residents erected an impressive cross-shaped memorial to Marie Toulinguet that looks out into Notre Dame Bay. These people had never heard her sing, yet knew the importance of reclaiming a great artist.

MARGOT DAVIES

Photo credit: CP.

She left the island at an early age, but the island never left her, and she always considered herself a Newfoundlander first and foremost. Margot "Margaret" Rhys Davies was born in St. John's (unfortunately we do not know the exact date) to the family of D. James Davies, a Welsh scientist who became the Justice of the Peace for Newfoundland in 1920. In 1930, Davies became Acting Commissioner for Newfoundland in London. Later, he was Trade Commissioner for Newfoundland. Davies moved his family to London around 1934, when Margot was probably in early adolescence.

But Newfoundland, Margot's birthplace and childhood home, would play a central role in the rest of her life. It was at Bishop Spencer, her St. John's school, that she developed a love of drama, first acting in "A Midsummer Night's Dream." In London, she continued her education in drama at the Central School of Speech

Training and Dramatic Art. She acted with the Dublin Gate Company at the Westminster Theatre, and later with the Oxford Repertory Company. Some thought she had great promise.

But, in September 1939, everything changed in England as war with Germany was declared. Margot promptly gave up her acting career to devote herself to the war effort. She threw herself into helping her father in the Newfoundland Office in London. They formed the Newfoundland War Contingent and, within a few weeks, the War Comforts Committee, with Margot as Honorary Assistant Secretary.

When the Newfoundland troops—there would be 7,000 by war's end—began pouring into London, Margot was at their service. It was she who got them beds, cigarettes, socks, balaclavas and whatever else they needed or wanted, in spite of rationing. She sorted their mail, organized tours of London for them, and arranged parties and dances. She did her best to console those who were homesick, and she got medicines for those who were ill. She did all this from the Comforts Room at the Newfoundland Office. Her only telephone was up two flights of stairs.

Margot had always been hyperactive, and now her boundless energy served her well. She wrote to a friend in September 1941: "I am as busy as ever in the Comforts Room! The boys come in 'thick and fast,' but it is all very pleasant—just like a big party everyday. They are so nice, too. I feel desperately sorry for some of the poor sailors who get endless stretches of leave with only enough money to keep them alive."

In 1940, Maxwell Littlejohn of St. John's started the BBC radio program "Calling from Britain to Newfoundland." In April 1941, Margot became its host, a position she occupied until her death thirty-one years later. The fifteen-minute show was broadcast on Monday and Wednesday mornings, initially via short-wave, to Newfoundland, and later on the CBC network. Those who didn't own radios went to the homes of their neighbours who did, to hear the program.

"Hello, Newfoundland, this is Margot Davies calling for the BBC London!" Margot's cheerful voice, with its light Welsh tones, rang out. Listeners heard the grave chimes of Big Ben, and then the terrible news of the Blitz pummelling British cities night after night. There was other news, too—anything that might be of interest to Newfoundlanders. This was the magazine format that aired on Mondays.

On Wednesdays, the program followed another format: Newfoundland servicemen read poetry, sang songs, and sent messages to their worried parents and wives back home. Former *Evening Telegram* columnist Jack White, a fan of "Calling Newfoundland," described both formats as "very emotional."

Margot did all the work associated with the program. She wrote the scripts and organized the troops, going here and there in London to fetch them and bring them to the studio. Taping a regular program during the worst of the war years was not always easy, but the host of "Calling Newfoundland" was nonchalant about it. She once remarked, "Generally there was a raid on outside, but usually it passed off in nice time for us all to get home."

Although she now had a full-time job in running the radio program, Margot continued assisting the Newfoundland Office, especially the Comforts Room. She was the main point of contact for any serviceman or -woman, and everyone coming overseas from Newfoundland knew her. Her efforts did not go unnoticed. Although she was still quite young, on January 1, 1941, she was made a Member of the Order of the British Empire (MBE) for "work in connection with the Newfoundland forces overseas."

Margot's intense focus on others extended well beyond her fellow Newfoundlanders. She befriended penniless students, people made homeless, and drug addicts. Over the years, she frequently handed the microphone to unknown poets so that they might have a chance at recognition. She cared nothing whatsoever for the material, and even less for social status, although she came from a family which included some members who were titled (her sister was Lady Bagge).

Her disinterest in the material led her to and then was reinforced by Christian Science, the religion founded by Mary Baker Eddy, to which she became deeply committed. Margot was very religious. She was constantly in dialogue with her faith, as revealed in her poems. One of her sonnets reads:

> For one brief moment I see all, and know
> How vast God is, how small a thing am I;
> He fills the earth, the ocean, and the sky,
> He *is* the world, one huge, one perfect whole,
> He is the throbbing Universe of Soul...

Margot had started writing poetry as a schoolgirl in St. John's. She also loved to recite it. "I love words," she once told Newfoundland artist Rae Perlin.

One of Margot's friends was G. Wilson Knight, a British literary critic and a former professor of English at the University of Toronto in the 1930s. They met in London and, being lovers of the theatre, corresponded afterwards. (It was one of Margot's habits to stay up till almost dawn writing letters.) She frequently sent Knight poems with her letters, which he saved. Some forty-five of these were published in 1981, in the slim volume *Calling Newfoundland*. Knight compares the poems to the simpler poems of Blake. In them we see joy, anxiety, and a living faith in God and the eternal. In Newfoundland, the book was sold through the Royal Canadian Legion for $5.95 plus postage.

The war ended, but Margot's radio program continued on a weekly basis, airing now on Sunday mornings. She did not want to give up, and her audience did not want her to, either. So, she sought out Newfoundlanders living in England—there were many in every corner—to speak to their families and friends back home. Her Christmas broadcasts were a highlight of the year. She invited about 100 Newfoundlanders and their families—children, grandchildren, and even great-grandchildren—to Bush House, home of the BBC, to send messages home on Christmas Day. The program always concluded with "The Ode to Newfoundland." Though Margot was not musical, the rendition was always a moving one.

> "Hello, Newfoundland, this is Margot Davies calling for the BBC London!" Margot's cheerful voice, with its light Welsh tones, rang out.

In 1961, on the twentieth anniversary of "Calling Newfoundland," Margot returned to Newfoundland at the invitation of the CBC. She was wined and dined at Government House, she sailed to Bell Island, met many war veterans and old friends, and finally flew back to London from Gander. The *Evening Telegram* reported her triumphant return with the headline "Margot Davies continues her mission of love."

She died eleven years later, in her early fifties, apparently of the anorexia nervosa that plagued her all her life. Margot lived on coffee and cigarettes, and always appeared frail. She slept very little, yet was very energetic. In her day, the disease was less common and less understood than it is now.

Margot's many friends remembered her phenomenal memory for words, people, faces and injuries. Wilson Knight wrote that she was "fun sparkling above the depths." She died, he said, "burnt out with devotion." At her memorial service at St. Martin's-in-the-Fields in Trafalgar Square, London, Sir Charles Curran, Director-

General of the BBC, recalled in his eulogy the proprietary way Newfoundlanders spoke about Margot and her program. Premier Joseph Smallwood read the lesson at the service and said she was "a legend, respected, and revered."

Back in Newfoundland, St. John's City Council named Davies Place, south of Brookfield Road, after Margot not long after her death. Maxwell Littlejohn instituted a memorial fund to erect a plaque in her honour. Today, the plaque can be seen in Confederation Building, having been unveiled by then Lieutenant-Governor Gordon Winter. It reads, from the well-loved prayer of St. Francis of Assissi, in part:

> Lord grant that we may seek rather to comfort
> than to be comforted.
> That where there is sadness, we may bring hope.
> And where there are shadows, we may bring light...

NEWFOUNDLAND FOLK RENAISSANCE

Traditional Newfoundland folk music is a rich heritage involving English, French, Irish and Scottish influences. The ethnicity of the music often depends on the area of the island, but sometimes Newfoundland music can create a unique blending of several early European folk traditions.

By its very nature, folk music is not written down, a fact which once put its survival in severe jeopardy. The emergence first of gramophone records in the late nineteenth and early twentieth centuries, and then radio, almost wiped out traditional Newfoundland music.

Folk music survives because the tunes are constantly played in households and during informal dances and parties. This way, it is passed from generation to generation. When something comes to take its place, a community or area can lose its folk tradition.

In the late 1960s and '70s, a sudden revival of interest in folk music in Newfoundland, spurred by a new generation of musicians like Figgy Duff and Kelly Russell, focused a new attention on traditional music. Folklorists were intent on finding and preserving the old musical craft from which the new bands derived their material. Suddenly, there was a market for some of the dedicated and talented traditional folk musicians who, though lauded in their own local scenes for many years, had yet to reach a wider audience.

Rufus Guinchard, Emile Benoit and Minnie White are three such musicians.

Rufus Guinchard (left) performing with Emile Benoit at the St. John's Folk Festival. Photo credit: Centre for Newfoundland Studies.

RUFUS GUINCHARD was born in Daniel's Harbour in September 1899, just months before the turn of the century. He learned to play the fiddle from uncles and great-uncles, who had themselves learned in the 1840s and '50s. His style—happily captured on TV in the 1980s—was therefore in part a record of the earliest Newfoundland folk music.

Guinchard's fiddling, however, was highly original, even right down to the way he held his instrument. As a child, Guinchard had been shy about being seen or overheard as he practised. Young Rufus had learned to play while staring out of the window, so he would be warned if anyone was approaching the house. He developed a unique way of holding the fiddle, cradling it on his right shoulder so he could look over his left. He also gripped the bow in the middle, the only way his child-sized arms could hold the adult instrument belonging to his father.

Guinchard quickly gained a local reputation in the Hawkes Bay area, where his family had moved. He was in constant demand for local dances. Telephone service was almost unknown. When his services were needed in West Coast communities like Cow Head or Parson's Pond, Guin-

> ... Guinchard would receive requests via telegraph. He would make his way, usually by foot, with his fiddle in hand.

chard would receive requests via telegraph. He would make his way, usually by foot, with his fiddle in hand.

Throughout his fiddling career, Guinchard composed many of his own tunes, and in line with the folk tradition, rewrote his own versions of old tunes, giving them a different name.

Like most of his folk musician peers, Guinchard never attempted to make a living at his craft, but held a great many jobs in resource industries. He was a trapper, river guardian, cook in a logging camp, carpenter, and later a watchmen with the Department of Highways, a job from which he retired in 1968.

But it was in retirement that his reputation would suddenly burst upon a provincial, then national, and finally international stage. Folklorists Al Pittman and Wilf Wareham persuaded Guinchard to perform for students at Memorial University. When it was clear his performance had made a splash, other invitations soon followed. Although in his seventies, Guinchard soon became part of a band, The Breakwater Boys, which included Clyde Rose, Pat and Joe Byrne, and Baxter Wareham. During his time with The

In her column, Marjorie Doyle remembered Guinchard as "an engaging personality and performer." Musical partner Kelly Russell wrote a 1981 biography entitled *Rufus Guinchard, The Man and His Music*, and an hour-long TV special by Red Ochre Productions captured not only Guinchard's musical technique, but his reminiscences of his early life in Daniel's Harbour and Hawkes Bay.

Breakwater Boys, Guinchard made a solo recording, *Rufus Guinchard—Newfoundland Fiddler.*

Guinchard's reputation and standing as a folk musician continued to grow after The Breakwater Boys split up in the late 1970s. In 1980, he teamed up with Kelly Russell on a Canadian tour and went to France and the U.S. He also travelled as far afield as Japan and Australia. In 1982, he released an LP, *Rufus Guinchard—Step Tunes and Doubles.* In 1986, he was given the Order of Canada for his work toward the "revival of the art of fiddling."

When Rufus Guinchard died in September 1990 in Corner Brook, a day after his ninety-first birthday, he was at the height of his fame. He was kindly remembered, not only by his wife Carrie and nine children, but also by the large and ever-growing circle of fans who had sought his music and company in the final decade of his life.

EMILE BENOIT, eccentric, engaging and irrepressible, was an all-around entertainer as well as fiddler. Combining his musicianship with the extrovert charm of a raconteur, Benoit was the ultimate in showmanship, and in later years would be a crucial part of the resurgence in Newfoundland's traditional music.

Born in Black Duck Siding on the Port au Port Peninsula in 1913, the French Newfoundlander was considered a master of the instrument by the time he was sixteen years old. When he was eight years old, he had begged his father to make him a violin. His father carved a rudimentary instrument out of pieces of juniper and catgut, and Benoit recalled how "my little heart was beating with gladness."

Like Guichard, Benoit was soon in great demand at parties and weddings. He later recalled how he bought his favourite violin when he was seventeen years old. "I got that...from an old woman. She was married to a Scotch, and I got that for thirty-five dollars. It took me a year to pay for it."

Never learning to read or write beyond Grade 3, Benoit had an eclectic career outside music until he was discovered outside his own local area in 1970. He had been a woodsman and fisherman, as well as his community's unofficial dentist and doctor. He is credited with saving his sister and her breached baby, and he was one of the bay's "traditional" dentists. "I pulled a hundred and thirty-five teeth," he once said, "and after that I lost count."

Benoit's official public debut came when he was fifty-seven years old, in Stephenville. Gathering a warm reception, he went on to appear on French and English TV and radio. He recorded three albums, and once claimed to have written 200 original tunes in his head, mostly in the jig-and-reel idiom. Some of these were recorded by Kelly Russell, Figgy Duff, Jim Payne and the Wonderful Grand Band.

Benoit became part of the Newfoundland folk renaissance and, by 1980, had also established a career as an internationally known artist playing in England, Norway, Wales and France, which had an special meaning for him as the land of his ancestors.

His stature was acknowledged by the province's university when Memorial gave him an honorary doctorate in 1988, and, in 1992, the year of his death, he was inducted into the Newfoundland and Labrador Arts Hall of Honour.

> "I admire myself too...for the way I does it and the way I compose and everything. I'm not learning anything off you, I'm learning it from myself—it could be good and it could be bad." Emile Benoit (*Sunday Express*).

His legacy is in highlighting the French side of Newfoundland's fiddling tradition, and in expressing the all-around vibrancy and colour that was often

His father carved a rudimentary instrument out of pieces juniper and catgut, and Benoit recalled how "my little heart was beating with gladness."

historically part of his instrument. He was aptly described by Mary Lynk in the *Sunday Express* as a "simple earthy person," and by Gerald Thomas, professor of French and Folklore at MUN, as possessing "a genuine charm that was very engaging, very simple." Although the wish was not acted upon, Benoit once expressed a desire that, when he died, he should be buried in a human-sized fiddle case.

Shane Kelly photo.

MINNIE WHITE, known as "the first lady of the accordion," was a musical force to be reckoned with. Giving up her instrument to marry and raise six children, she started playing again at middle age, then financed the recording and arranged distribution for her five albums. The last of these, *The Hills of Home*, was nominated in two categories of the East Coast Music Awards.

It was a tribute to her great talent and indomitable spirit that, when she died at eighty-five years old on December 15, 2001, the *Globe and Mail* ran a full-page obituary.

Mary Agnes Hopkins was born in St. Alban's in 1916. She started playing secretly when she was eight years old, teaching herself on her father's accordion when he was out of the house. When her father found this out, he immediately began instructing her. White favoured the two-row accordion, which produced a softer, gentler sound than the more common four-stop accordion.

When she was sixteen years old, she took a job as a housekeeper in the Codroy Valley. From that time onward, the soft, green mountains of the area—a landscape very much in contrast with the rugged coasts of much of the island—became part of her musical inspiration. "People always said they could follow the valley if they listened to my songs," she would later say.

> "People always said they could follow the valley if they listened to my songs."

But music was to come second to family life. In 1937, at the age of twenty-one, Minnie married Richard White, a farmer and fishermen's guide. They settled down in the Codroy Valley community of Tompkins and raised six children.

It was 1960 before White was able to pick up her accordion again, and she began to attract a local following, playing at the Starlite Motel. It was soon obvious there was something special about White's playing. "She had a neat, clean sound as a result of her precise timing," musician Jim Payne recalled in her *Globe and Mail* obituary. "Every note fitted into a slot."

White was very much admired, but people also found her intimidating. At the Starlite Motel, she would appear always in full evening gown, and, unlike her peers, she did not improvise in performance. In fact, she was something of a stickler. Jim Payne recalled that "if a band member didn't take it seriously or used vulgarity, she fired them."

> "...if a band member didn't take it seriously or used vulgarity, she fired them."

Throughout the thirteen years she played a regular gig at the Starlite Motel, White's reputation was on the rise outside the area, too. She augmented her growing reputation by undertaking a series of albums, starting with *Newfoundland's First Lady of the Accordion* in 1973. She funded the project herself and handled her own distribution, and the album was successful enough to finance a second, *Midnight Watch*, which in turn was followed by *I Played it My Way*, and then the East Coast Music Award–nominated *The Hills of Home*.

In 1993, Minnie was given the ultimate accolade of the

> Unlike many of the folk musicians, Minnie also drew influence from every major Newfoundland ethnicity: Scottish (of the Codroy Valley), Irish, English and French (from the Port au Port Peninsula). She would learn songs from other musicians, and also wrote many of her own.

Order of Canada. By now, sadly, she had developed osteoporosis in her shoulders, which would prevent her from playing in the last years of her life. In 1999, she was presented with the Dr. Helen Creighton Lifetime Achievement Award. Even though she had not played for some time, when Minnie White died nearly three years later, she was still a highly celebrated musician.

COMEDY WITHOUT MALICE

TED RUSSELL

Photo credit: Elizabeth Miller.

Although Ted Russell regarded himself as a hobbyist rather than a professional writer, his influence as a Newfoundland literary figure was both vital and widespread. With the creation of the mythical setting of Pigeon Inlet, and characters who were humorous and whimsical, but never buffoons, Russell brought a dignity and clear-sightedness to writing about rural Newfoundland that served as an important focus for emerging writers of the 1950s and beyond.

Born June 27, 1904, in the small community of Coley's Point in Conception Bay, Russell was steeped in the rural tradition that for much of his adult life stood on the brink of change. He was educated at Bishop Feild College in St. John's, and, although he left school at sixteen, went straight out into rural Newfoundland as a teacher. He taught in Pass Island (reputedly the model for Pigeon Inlet), Harbour Breton,

Millertown, Channel and Fogo. After twelve years teaching, he went back to upgrade his education at Memorial University College, and, then in 1933, still without a degree, became part of the teaching staff of Bishop Feild.

In 1935, he married Dora Oake and, over a span of twenty years, they were to have four girls and one boy. In the same year as his marriage, Russell was appointed to the Newfoundland magistracy, in which capacity he served in Springdale, Harbour Breton and Bonne Bay. In 1943, he was appointed Director of Co-operatives within the Commission of Government, a move that undoubtedly thrust him into a prominent position for the great political changes which were to take place after the war. Then, in 1949, he was elected into Newfoundland's first House of Assembly, and became Minster of Natural Resources.

It was in this brief and uncomfortable time as part of Joey Smallwood's cabinet that Russell's political philosophy came into clear focus. He believed in economic growth and modernization, but not of the kind that relied an excess of non-traditional and largely speculative new industries. It was largely over this issue that Russell resigned on March 24, 1951, sitting as an Independent until the November election, which he did not contest. Following his departure from politics, he became an insurance salesman for Crown Life.

In 1966, Ted Russell published his political memoirs in *The Evening Telegram*. It was extremely damning to Joey Smallwood. Example extract: "His open bragging and blatant boasting about how much he gained from Confederation did him a lot, but did Newfoundland a great disservice. But he didn't mind that. He always played on the ignorance and greed of Newfoundlanders. Take, for example, unemployment insurance for self-employed fishermen.... Catch insurance—yes! But unemployment insurance no! We taught our fishermen to fish for stamps."

During the next few years, Russell began to distill his feelings about rural Newfoundland into a series of plays and dramatic monologues, which were aired on the CBC's popular Fishermen's Broadcast from 1953 onward. *The Chronicles of Uncle Mose*, set in the fictional outport of Pigeon Inlet, was an instant success, and people in Newfoundland identified with the verity of the characters and the gentle humour. Over a period of eight years, 600 eight-minute monologues were broadcast, and Russell himself would read over the microphone, "in character" as Uncle Mose.

Broadcaster Rex Murphy has compared the Pigeon Inlet stories to the work of English writer P.G. Wodehouse, commenting that "the humour of both is utterly without malice or sneer."

In fact, the gentleness of Russell's humour and his characterizations drew some criticism at the time, although some were quick to defend. Harold Horwood in the *Evening Telegram* commented on a CBC radio broadcast of Russell's play *The Holdin' Ground*, saying, "It lasted a full hour, with not an unkind word from anybody. No one was murdered.... No one was robbed or battered. No one...screamed or indulged in violent language.... In spite of that, people...were even lavish in their praise. This...may indicate that the public taste for mayhem is not so insatiable as the leaders of the entertainment industry believe."

Russell himself explained the lack of villains in his work by linking it to his philosophy: "...it all depends on whether you consider human beings as good or evil. I wrote about the people as I knew them—with their little faults, but basically good people."

While using wit and colourful characterizations, Russell was considered successful in avoiding stereotypes or clowns. "He wasn't afraid of giving 'the folk' real minds," Rex Murphy has commented.

Between 1954 and 1957, Russell also wrote eight plays, using the same setting of Pigeon Inlet and the same characters as *The Chronicles of Uncle Mose*. These were broadcast on radio and also performed by theatre groups. The most famous, *Holdin' Ground*, won the Provincial Drama Festival when performed by the Northcliffe Drama Club in 1956.

In the early 1960s, Russell turned away from Pigeon Inlet and went back to Memorial University in order to finish his degree. Graduating in 1965 at the age of sixty-one, he joined the English department. In this new role as educator, his wide experience and warmth made him uncommonly gifted. As Patrick O' Flaherty remembers (quoted in Elizabeth Miller's biography of Russell), "...he was a superbly gifted teacher, with a common touch, a gentle sense of humour, and a fund of homely wisdom which never ceased to enhance his pupils."

His standing and influence was acknowledged by an honorary degree in 1973. He died on October 16, 1977. Although only a portion of *The Chronicles of Uncle Mose* scripts and recordings have survived (radio broadcasting was until recently considered a transient medium, and many valuable recordings have been lost or thrown away), Russell's legacy has continued to be celebrated after

---

"Jethro is not exactly the tidiest fellow in the world...I better explain what Jethro's face looks like with two or three weeks' whisker on it.... The only thing I can compare it to is the North West corner of Gull Marsh, just after you've got over the barren part and you're gettin' near to the foothills where we go for firewood. Well that section of the marsh is all spotted—mostly bare spots with here and there a clump of ground juniper or a small patch of alders or a few blueberry bushes—or an old gnarled stump—stuff like that." From *The Chronicles of Uncle Mose*, quoted in *The Life and Times of Ted Russell* (Elizabeth Miller)

> "I wrote about the people as I knew them—with their little faults, but basically good people."

his death. In 1981, his daughter Elizabeth Miller published a biography, *The Life and Times of Ted Russell.* Several of his plays and monologues have been collected and published. In 1985, CBC began a television series, *Yarns from Pigeon Inlet,* based on Ted Russell's work. In 2005, Flanker Press of St. John's published a revised biography of Ted Russell, *Uncle Mose: The Life of Ted Russell,* by Elizabeth Miller.

Russell himself saw his writing as a record of a changing world. "I did my writing at a time when I saw that the things I valued were just beginning to die," he once said "I wrote about them while they were still there. The reason I have given up writing about them is that it is no longer there."

And therein lies the poignancy of Russell's legacy.

CONFEDERATION-BOUND

JOSEPH ROBERTS SMALLWOOD

Photo credit: Smallwood Heritage Foundation.

Labour activist, political idealist, journalist, father of Confederation, and Newfoundland's first and longest-serving premier (from 1949–1972), Joey Smallwood remains a name to conjure deep emotions. Adored by some and loathed by others, he is probably Newfoundland's most undisputed icon. To his admirers, he is Newfoundland's saviour, a genuine liberal socialist who brought Newfoundland into Canada with its prosperity and its welfare state. To his enemies, he was a dangerous fanatic and tyrant, Canada and Britain's spy during the war, the villain who sold Newfoundland off to the highest bidder in 1948, and then thwarted democratic discussion and healthy dissent.

Smallwood was born in Gambo in 1900, to Charles and Mary Ellen (Devanna) Smallwood. The Smallwood family were culturally middle class, but economically poor. Joseph's father, Charles, was an alcoholic, a harsh reality which gave the Smallwood home a sense of instability in Joey's early years. "I remember scores of incidents that occurred in our home when my father was drunk, but they are not pleasant to remember or tell," Smallwood wrote in his memoirs. The father's drinking problem instilled a sense of a "secret shame" in the family. And it also meant his father did a great deal of moving from job to job. He worked as a salesman, in construction and also in farm-related work, reflecting Charles's own heritage as the son of a P.E.I. farmer. Soon after Joseph's birth, the family moved to St. John's.

At the age of ten, through the charity of his well-to-do Uncle Fred, Joey became a boarding student of Bishop Fcild College. "I was almost speechless with happiness," Smallwood recalled. The private school meant, in his own words, that Joey was "placed ...cheek-by-jowl with the scions of many of the wealthy merchants in St. John's." The experience was a profound one for Smallwood, igniting at once an inferiority complex and a determination to distinguish himself.

It was in this setting that the young Joey first tried out his leadership skills, organizing his fellow students in a successful strike against the canteen food at Bishop Feild. He found that he could overcome his diminutive size and also his lack of family stature by having his peers focus instead upon his indomitable spirit. He started to build what he would later call his "unqualified, unwavering, unquestioned confidence in myself, my potential, and my destiny." Smallwood had also begun to show an interest in radical politics. Socialism, he said, appealed to him because he "hated injustice and cruelty and felt certain that wealth was most unfairly distributed."

Another influence may have shaped Joey's ability to move a crowd. His mother had begun to take an interest in the Pentecostal Church and had taken her son to revival meetings to witness the energy and emotion on display there. Joey's declamatory, repetitive and emotional speaking style may have owed a great deal to the revivalist spirit.

In 1915, having proved a troublesome pupil, Smallwood left school to start work in the printing business. So started a lifelong obsession with the written word. He worked first with the St. John's newspaper the *Plaindealer*, then the *Spectator*, then the *Daily News*, before moving on to the *Evening Telegram* as a reporter. Now that he was in the workforce, he continued his socialist activities by helping in his spare time to produce the *Industrial Worker*.

Smallwood's horizons were soon to expand geographically, too. Working for various newspapers, he moved to Halifax, then Boston, and finally to New York, where he began working for the socialist newspaper *Call* as a reporter.

Over the next few years, Smallwood divided his time between Newfoundland and New York, living in dire poverty in the big city, but building and storing a knowledge base of political movements and their relationship with impoverished people. He studied intensely. "I spent unnumbered hours," he recalled in his memoirs, "in the library of the Rand School of Social Science in New York, dipping into what must have been the world's greatest collections of Socialist literature."

He worked periodically for newspapers, but threw himself with increasing fervour into left-wing politics, speaking for the Socialist Party in the 1924 presidential election.

Back in Newfoundland, he began to bring his new-found confidence to labour activities, successfully reorganizing Local 63 of the International Brotherhood of Pulp, Sulphite and Paper Mill Workers in Grand Falls, and increasing membership from 100 to 900. He also formed Newfoundland's first Federation of Labour, an umbrella group for all Newfoundland unions, although the organization was short-lived.

Then came Smallwood's most legendary labour coup, organizing the province's 600 railway sectionmen against a wage cut threatened by management. The feat of signing up the railway workers required him to walk vast distances of the enormous island-long railway track. But he succeeded, and when he finally met railway officials at Avondale, he had momentum and a clear moral right to address the management. He succeeded in getting management to back down.

Such victories did not go unnoticed in the press, and one of Smallwood's public addresses prompted lawyer and sportsman George Ayre to publicly call the idea of Smallwood one day being a leader "...a glorious prospect!"

It was while engaged in union activities in 1926 in Corner Brook Smallwood first met his future wife, Clara Oates. He started his own weekly newspaper, the *Labour Outlook*, for railway workers,

Then came Smallwood's most legendary labour coup, organizing the province's 600 railway sectionmen against a wage cut threatened by management.

and continued to play a vital and dynamic role in the labour movement, but at the same time tipped his hat at the Liberal Party by suggesting that, if it could become reforming and compassionate enough, then a Labour Party would not be necessary.

A year later, after Smallwood established yet another newspaper, the *Humber Herald*, in Corner Brook, he sought the Liberal nomination for the first time, but lost and had to contend with being a district campaign manager instead. Remaining in an advisory role for the Liberals, he became a close confidant of the Prime Minister Richard Squires and agreed to oversee a liberal newspaper, the *Watchdog*, in 1930.

Smallwood was even by Squires's side in April 1932 when an angry mob, squeezed by the Great Depression, invaded the Colonial Building, demanding the Prime Minister's resignation. Squires resigned and had to flee the building by a series of back doors and routes through people's houses. The incident seems to have marked a sea change in Smallwood's outlook. Running in the subsequent election, he argued for the first time that Newfoundland could no longer politically make it on its own and needed "a long political holiday," or suspension of Responsible Government.

In the event, Smallwood proved a prophet for the first time. A commission on Newfoundland's constitutional future concluded with a reversion to a Commission of Government. Until further notice, Newfoundland would be governed from London.

Although labelled a traitor in some quarters, Smallwood continued to believe that Newfoundland needed the umbrella of a more powerful nation.

In the political wilderness of the Commission of Government

Although labelled a traitor in some quarters, Smallwood continued to believe that Newfoundland needed the umbrella of a more powerful nation.

years, Smallwood spent the time conquering new media and industries. In 1937, he edited and co- authored *The Book of Newfoundland*, a treasury of Newfoundlandia, which was intended to "restore the faith of Newfoundlanders in their country." He is known to have sold volumes on the side of the road from the trunk of his car.

Under the pseudonym "The Barrelman," Smallwood started writing a column for the *Daily News* in 1942. Like *The Book of Newfoundland*, these columns collected nuggets of information about Newfoundland and were, in his words, "devoted to the glorification of Newfoundland and everything within it."

The popularity of this column led radio station VONF to give Smallwood his own radio show, under the same Barrelman moniker. In the later war years, Smallwood's voice, opinions and personality became widely familiar among the majority of Newfoundlanders.

This was an advantage that would aid Smallwood considerably when his political career began again with the National Convention in 1946.

During the war years, Smallwood reclaimed his P.E.I. farming heritage by importing pigs from P.E.I. and starting a highly successful hog farm, at first near St. John's, and then Gander.

In December 1945, British Prime Minister Clement Attlee announced there would be a National Convention in St. John's, through which forty-five elected Newfoundland representatives would explore all the options for Newfoundland's constitutional future and report back to London with proposals that might be voted on in a referendum. Smallwood was determined to become part of this, and very quickly made up his mind that Newfoundland should join Canada. As early as March 1946, Smallwood began writing articles for the *Daily News*, publishing this view. He ran in Bonavista Centre for election into the National Convention and won easily.

During the National Convention debates, Smallwood and his chief ally, Gordon Bradley, argued repeatedly that Confederation with Canada should be on the ballot of any forthcoming referendum to decide Newfoundland's fate. Peter Cashin was a main political adversary. The debate became more and more polarized, swinging from advocates of Confederation with Canada to return to Responsible Government. In the summer of 1947, Smallwood and Bradley successfully argued that they should be sent as a delegation to Ottawa with authority to negotiate theoretical terms for Confederation. When the terms arrived late in the year, the National Convention rejected them from inclusion on the ballot. Smallwood responded by firing up listeners on VONF and urging them to petition the British Government to impose the option on the ballot. Letters came by the tens of thousands.

The first referendum, held on June 3, 1948, included three options—a continuation of Commission of Government, return to Responsible Government, and Confederation with Canada. The first option performed poorly enough to be dropped. Between the two other options, Responsible Government nosed ahead.

The second referendum was held on July 22, and was now a straight battle between Responsible Government and Confederation with Canada. This time Confederation inched ahead, winning with 52.3% of the vote.

Views about Smallwood often revolve around the fateful vote which took Newfoundland into Canada and propelled him into power. One theme often repeated by his critics was the way in which Smallwood and the Confederation camp instilled fear into Newfoundlanders, suggesting they could not make it alone. Certainly the case for Responsible Government was ruthlessly burlesqued in the Confederate propaganda which suggested only poverty and destruction awaited such a path.

Among some skeptics, suspicion even hovers over the extent of Smallwood's communication with both Canada and Britain, not only during, but even before, the National Convention. Some modern historians, such as John Fitzgerald, suggest the whole thing was a "done deal" and the referenda were merely formalities designed to rubber-stamp a decision already made. It was well known, for instance, that Great Britain was actively trying to shed all remnants of its Empire by 1946, and had no intention of keeping Newfoundland. The inclusion of Commission of Government on the first ballot was surely then only a formality.

David Benson traces the "decision" for New-

> **FIRST REFERENDUM, JUNE 3, 1948**
>
> Commission of Government—14.3 %
> Responsible Government—44.5 %
> Confederation—41.1 %

In the second referendum, Commission of Government was dropped and Confederation won by 52.3% of the vote.

foundland to join Canada to as early as 1941, when U.S. President Franklin Roosevelt suggested to Canadian Prime Minster W.L.M. King that Canada take over Newfoundland. According to Benson, King agreed, but told the president it should wait until the end of the war.

So, was Smallwood just an agent of the larger powers who were seeking to divide up the smaller states after the war? If so, what of the episode in which he pressed VONF listeners to write London, insisting that alignment with Canada be put on the ballot? Was this a mere publicity stunt designed to fan the growing Confederate flame? Did it have the tacit support of the British and Canadian governments?

Such questions remain part of a fierce and ongoing debate, and even the subject of the movie *Secret Nation*, which explores the conspiracy theory in detail, including the notions of missing ballots in the final vote. Perhaps the biggest stumbling block of the conspiracy theory is the strength and determination of Smallwood's character, which was quite capable of taking charge of political situations and creating change without outside interference.

"Most Newfoundlanders seem to think their country's post-war existence was unique. In fact, it was commonplace. Newfoundland was just one of dozens of small countries to change hands as the victors reorganized the global map," David Benson, *TickleAce*, special Confederation 50 issue.

SELECTED
BIBLIOGRAPHY

Ackroyd, Peter (2000) *London: The Biography*. London: Chatto & Windus.

Author Unknown (July, 1913) Newfoundland's Most Successful Seal Killer. *Newfoundland Quarterly*, 13 (1): 30, 32.

Bartlett, Robert A. (1916) *The Last Voyage of the* Karluk, *flagship of Vilhhalmar Stefansson's Canadian Arctic Expedition of 1913–1916*. Boston: Small, Maynard & Co.

Beaton, Marilyn, and Jeanette Walsh (2002) *From the Voices of Nurses: An Oral History of Newfoundland Nurses Who Graduated Prior to 1920*. St. John's: Jesperson Publishing.

Belbin, Victoria Page Sparkes (April, 1996) Midwifery and Rural Newfoundland Health Care 1920–1950: A case study of Nurse Myra Bennett, nurse midwife. Honours dissertation. St. John's: Memorial University.

Benoit, Cecilia (1991) *Midwives in Passage: the modernization of maternity care*. St. John's: Institute for Social and Economic Research, Memorial University.

Benson, David (n.d.) Dunch Arses and Cargo Cults: Newfoundland as a Province of Canada. *TickleAce*, (37): 70–84.

Brown, Cassie with Harold Horwood (1972) *Death On the Ice: The Great Newfoundland Sealing Disaster of 1914*. Toronto: Doubleday.

Brown, Cassie (1996) Death March: The Story of a Sealing Disaster. In *The Caribou Disaster and Other Short Stories*. St. John's: Flanker Press, pp. 6–24.

Brown, Cassie (2003) *A Winter's Tale: The Wreck of the Florizel.* St. John's: Flanker Press.

Butler, Paul (2004) *Easton.* St. John's: Flanker Press.

Cadigan, Sean (1995) *Hope and Deception in Conception Bay: merchant-settler relations in Newfoundland, 1785–1855.* Toronto: University of Toronto Press.

Crellin, John K. (1994) *Home Medicine: The Newfoundland Experience.* Toronto: McGill- Queen's University Press.

Cuff, Robert (1983) On the Cars: Winter Logging on the Bonavista Peninsula (1911–1949). *Newfoundland Quarterly,* 79 (2): 13–17.

Davies, Margot (1981) *Calling Newfoundland. Poems, 1940–1941.* G. Wilson Knight, ed. North Walsham, Norfolk: Warren House Press.

Drodge, Eldon (2000) *Jackman: the courage of Captain William Jackman.* St. John's: Jesperson Publishing.

Drodge, Eldon (2001) *Kerrivan: a novel based on the legend of the Society of Masterless Men.* St. John's: Jesperson Publishing.

Duff, Shannie (Sept., 1974) A Brief Biography of William Carson, M.D. *Newfoundland Medical Association Newsletter,* 16 (4): 28–35.

Duncan, Norman (1905) *Dr. Grenfell's parish: the deep sea fishermen.* London: Hodder & Stoughton.

Fardy, Bernard F. (1988) *Demasduit: A Native Newfoundlander.* St. John's: Creative Book Publishing.

Feltham, John (1995) *Sealing Steamers.* St. John's: Harry Cuff Publications.

Green, H. Gordon (1973) *Don't Have Your Baby in the Dory.* Montreal: Harvest House.

Grenfell, Wilfred T. (1919) *Labrador Doctor: the autobiography of Sir Wilfred Grenfell.* Boston: Houghton Mifflin.

Hancock, W. Gordon (1989) *Soe longe as there comes noe women: Origins of English Settlement in Newfoundland.* St. John's: Breakwater Books.

Hanrahan, Maura (2003) The Lasting Breach: The Omission of Aboriginal People from the Terms of Union between Newfoundland and Canada. St. John's: Royal Commission on Renewing and Strengthening Our Place in Canada, Government of Newfoundland and Labrador.

Harrington, Michael (n.d.) *The Prime Ministers of Newfoundland.*

Horwood, Andrew (1971) *Newfoundland Ships and Men: Schooner, Square Rigger, Captains and Crews.* St. John's: The Marine Researchers.

Horwood, Harold and Edward Butts (1984) *Pirates and Outlaws of Canada, 1610–1932.* Toronto: Doubleday.

Horwood, Harold (1977) *Bartlett: the great explorer.* Toronto: Doubleday.

Kean, Abram (2000) *Old and Young Ahead.* St. John's: Flanker Press.

Mannion, John J. (1977) Settlers and Traders in Western Newfoundland. In *Peopling of Newfoundland: Essays in Historical Geography.* ed. John Mannion, 234–75. St. John's: Institute of Social and Economic Research, Memorial University of Newfoundland.

Martin, Steve and Colin Sanger (1997) Matthew *Bonavista Bound.* St. John's: Breakwater Books.

Matthews, Keith (1988) *Lectures on the History of Newfoundland, 1500–1830.* St. John's: Breakwater Books.

McKinley, William Laird (1976) *Karluk: the great untold story of Arctic Exploration.* New York: St. Martin's Press.

Miller, Elizabeth Russell, ed. (2005) *Uncle Mose: The Life of Ted Russell.* St. John's: Flanker Press.

Miller, Elizabeth Russell, ed. (1984) *The Best of Ted Russell, No. 1, and Stories from Uncle Mose.* St. John's: Harry Cuff Publications.

Mowat, Farley and David Blackwood (1973) *Wake of the Great Sealers.* Toronto: Little, Brown and Company.

Moyles, R.G. (1975) *"Complaints is many and various, but the odd Divil likes it":* *Nineteenth Century View of Newfoundland.* Toronto: Peter Martin Associates.

Murray, Hilda Chaulk (1979) *More than Fifty Percent: a woman's life in a Newfoundland Outport.* St. John's: Breakwater Books.

Neary, Peter (1961) The French Shore Problem in Newfoundland. M.A. thesis, Memorial University of Newfoundland.

Noel, S.J.R. (1971) *Politics in Newfoundland.* Toronto: University of Toronto Press.

Nurse Myra Bennett Foundation Newsletter. May 2000.

Nurse Myra Bennett Foundation Newsletter. Vol. 1, Oct. 1999.

O'Flaherty, Patrick (1999) *Old Newfoundland: A History to 1843.* St. John's: Long Beach Press.

O'Flaherty, Patrick (April 30, 1981) In Search of William Carson. Paper presented to the Newfoundland Historical Society.

Peyton, Amy Louise (1983) *Nightingale of the North.* St. John's: Jesperson Publishing.

Prowse, Daniel W. (1895) *History of Newfoundland.* London: Macmillan and Co.

Ryan, Shannon (1986) *Fish Out of Water: The Newfoundland Saltfish Trade, 1814–1914.* St. John's: Breakwater Books.

Samuelson, Karl (1984) *Fourteen Men.* St. John's: Robinson-Blackmore.

Sexty, Robert and Sue Sexty (2000) Lady Sara Kirke: Canada's First Female Entrepreneur or One of Many? Montreal, Quebec: ASAC-IFSAM Conference.

Smallwood, Joseph R., editor in chief. *Encyclopedia of Newfoundland and Labrador*. Various editions. St. John's: Newfoundland Book Publishers.

Smallwood, Joseph R. (1967) *Dr. William Carson. The Newfoundland Reformer: his life, letters and speeches: raw material for a biography*. St. John's: Newfoundland Book Publishers.

Smith, Alex (2003) *The Grenfell I Knew*. St. John's: Flanker Press.

Smith, Philip E. (1987) In Winter Quarters. *Newfoundland Studies*, 3 (1): 1–36.

Story, G.M., W.J. Kirwin, and J.D.A. Widdowson (1982) *Dictionary of Newfoundland English*. Toronto: University of Toronto Press.

White, Marian Frances (1992) *The Finest Kind: women's voices from Newfoundland and Labrador*. St. John's: Creative Book Publishing.

White, Paula Maureen (1977) A Study of Patrick Morris's Political Rhetoric. Memorial University, St. John's: M.A. Thesis.

Whiteley, George (Nov. 15, 1937) Seal Hunter. *Maclean's Magazine*: 24, 50.

> **Note:** We also made extensive use of files at the Centre for Newfoundland Studies, Queen Elizabeth Library, Memorial University of Newfoundland, the *Evening Telegram* (now the *Telegram*), the *Daily News*, and other archived publications.

Look for Future Books by
Paul Butler and Maura Hanrahan
Featuring These Fascinating Historical Figures

"**Santu** was ten when she left Newfoundland—Taqamakuk—in 1847. She moved to Nova Scotia with her Beothuk father, Kop.... In 1872, on one of her trips home to Newfoundland, she had her picture taken at Badger Brook..."

"As a reformer, **William Coaker** showed his promise very early in life. At the age of thirteen, while still at school, he led a successful strike of boy employees at Bowrings, a large St. John's exporting firm."

"She once called Newfoundland 'the best country in the world for writers.' Yet novelist **Margaret Duley** never got the recognition in her native land that came naturally to her elsewhere..."

And Read About:

Black Bart, one of the island's most menacing pirates...; **Commodore Pearl**, who fought with the governor and passed himself off as an Admiral...; Newfoundland's War Hero **Tommy Ricketts**, the youngest ever recipient of the Victoria Cross...; **Betty Munn**, the little girl who inspired the Peter Pan statue in Bowring Park...

EASTON   ISBN 1-894463-64-1

Having just escaped the King's justice, notorious pirate Peter Easton arrives in St. John's harbour with ten well-armed ships. Knowing he is too powerful to be refused, Easton confidently invites the King's loyal fishing admiral, Richard Whitbourne, and his second-in-command, Captain Dawson, aboard his flagship *The Happy Adventure*. Insisting Whitbourne and Dawson are guests and not prisoners, Easton takes them by surprise, pulling anchor and setting sail with half his flotilla for the Caribbean.

Easton takes place in Newfoundland, the Caribbean and England. The story reflects a time when Newfoundland was crucial to trade and power, and when there was a very thin line between loyalty and piracy—a line that could be crossed in either direction in the blink of an eye.

STOKER'S SHADOW   ISBN 1-894463-32-3

(Short-listed for the 2004 Newfoundland and Labrador Book Award.)

"Paul Butler successfully accomplishes what few others have ever done: to weave together the disparate fabric of Gothic myth and modern revelation. The prose is lush, hypnotic and inviting and effectively merges the emerging social rhythms of 1920s London with the darker, more primeval forces of Bram Stoker's Transylvania. Stoker's Shadow is a stunning achievement that will doubtless gather to itself all praise." – J.S. Cook, author of *A Cold-Blooded Scoundrel*

THE SURROGATE SPIRIT   ISBN 0-921692-96-X

Walter Jefferson's spirit wrestles with two worlds, past and present, and tries to find an answer to the jigsaw puzzle of his life and death.

TSUNAMI: THE NEWFOUNDLAND
TIDAL WAVE DISASTER   ISBN 1-894463-63-3

(Short-listed for the 2005 Newfoundland and Labrador Book Award.)

Here is the dramatic, incredible story of the South Coast Disaster of 1929, the superhuman efforts of Nurse Dorothy Cherry to save the sick and dying, and Magistrate Hollett's tireless campaign to rebuild shattered lives and devastated communities.

THE DORYMAN   ISBN 1-894463-40-4

(Short-listed for the 2004 History and Heritage Award.)

The Doryman follows the story of Richard Hanrahan from age nine when he is ripped away from the safety and comfort of the schoolroom to the seasonal shore fishery on Newfoundland's south coast in the late 1800s. It is a compelling tale filled with spirited characters, tragedy and resilience, tidal waves and August gales.

A VERITABLE SCOFF: ISBN 1-894463-21-8
SOURCES ON FOODWAYS AND NUTRITION
IN NEWFOUNDLAND AND LABRADOR
(with Marg Ewtushik)

A Veritable Scoff presents summaries of 170 writings on Newfoundland and Labrador foodways and nutrition for the past several centuries.